Tacitus *Annals* I

The following titles are available from Bloomsbury for the OCR specifications in Latin and Greek, first teaching September 2016

Cicero *Pro Milone*: A Selection, with introduction by Lynn Fotheringham and commentary notes and vocabulary by Robert West

Ovid *Heroides*: A Selection, with introduction, commentary notes and vocabulary by John Godwin

Propertius, Tibullus and Ovid: A Selection of Love Poetry, with introduction, commentary notes and vocabulary by Anita Nikkanen

Seneca Letters: A Selection, with introduction, commentary notes and vocabulary by Eliot Maunder

Tacitus *Annals* I: A Selection, with introduction by Roland Mayer and commentary notes and vocabulary by Katharine Radice

Virgil *Aeneid* VIII: A Selection, with introduction, commentary notes and vocabulary by Keith Maclennan

Virgil *Aeneid* X: A Selection, with introduction, commentary notes and vocabulary by Christopher Tanfield

OCR Anthology for Classical Greek GCSE, covering the prescribed texts by Homer, Herodotus, Euripides, Lucian, Plato and Plutarch, edited by Judith Affleck and Clive Letchford

OCR Anthology for Classical Greek AS and A-level, covering the prescribed texts by Aristophanes, Homer, Plato, Sophocles, Thucydides and Xenophon, with introduction, commentary notes and vocabulary by Malcolm Campbell, Rob Colborn, Frederica Daniele, Ben Gravell, Sarah Harden, Steven Kennedy, Matthew McCullagh, Charlie Paterson, John Taylor and Claire Webster

Supplementary resources for these volumes can be found at
www.bloomsbury.com/OCR-editions
Please type the URL into your web browser and follow the instructions to access the Companion Website. If you experience any problems, please contact Bloomsbury at academicwebsite@bloomsbury.com

Tacitus *Annals* I:
A Selection

Chapters 3–7, 11–14, 16–30, 46–49

Introduction by Roland Mayer
Commentary notes and vocabulary by
Katharine Radice

Bloomsbury Academic
An imprint of Bloomsbury Publishing Plc

B L O O M S B U R Y
LONDON · OXFORD · NEW YORK · NEW DELHI · SYDNEY

Bloomsbury Academic

An imprint of Bloomsbury Publishing Plc

50 Bedford Square
London
WC1B 3DP
UK

1385 Broadway
New York
NY 10018
USA

www.bloomsbury.com

BLOOMSBURY and the Diana logo are trademarks of Bloomsbury Publishing Plc

First published 2016

British Library Cataloguing-in-Publication Data
A catalogue record for this book is available from the British Library.

ISBN: PB: 978-1-47426-598-0
ePub: 978-1-47426-599-7
ePDF: 978-1-47426-600-0

Library of Congress Cataloging-in-Publication Data
A catalog record for this book is available from the Library of Congress.

Typeset by RefineCatch Limited, Bungay, Suffolk
Printed and bound in Great Britain

Contents

Preface

This edition is designed to support students reading these sections of Tacitus in preparation for OCR's AS and A-Level examinations from June 2017 to 2019. (Please note this edition uses AS to refer indiscriminately to AS and the expected first year of A Level, i.e. Group 1.) In pithy, acerbic prose, Tacitus writes of the awkwardness and impact of the beginning of Tiberius' principate and the rebellions of opportunistic soldiers. This edition aims to provide an understanding of the significance of these events in the context of Roman history, and of the punchy vitality of Tacitus' prose.

The Introduction surveys the historical background, the impact of autocratic government, and the historical sources. The events of the accession of Tiberius and the mutinies abroad are summarized. The Roman historiographical tradition is then described, as is Tacitus' own career. Closer analysis of the extracts set for examination follows. The final section aims to promote appreciation of the quality and chief characteristics of Tacitus' extraordinary prose style and syntax.

The notes are primarily designed to help students understand the Latin accurately. Explanations are included of constructions not encountered at GCSE (especially so in the notes for the AS section), and idioms particular to Tacitus are highlighted and explained. Analysis of literary style, therefore, concentrates on aspects which might be lost in translation (the power of the impersonal passive, for example, or Tacitus' compressed and often surprising sentence structure). Aspects which shine through even after translation (such as emotional intensity, use of direct speech, construction of dramatic scenes, use of contrast, choice of detail, authorial comment etc), are typically not noted.

There is a comprehensive vocabulary; we have tried to offer basic meanings of the words in order to help general vocabulary learning, and also meanings which will suit the context of the words in this text. Since it is impossible to do justice to a word's meaning in a brief list, readers are strongly encouraged to make use of a full-sized dictionary.

Maps of Germany and Pannonia are provided, along with an index of persons and places. Members of the Imperial Family are separately listed, with notes on their relation to Augustus; the family tree will help readers negotiate this notoriously confusing family!

Roland Mayer wrote the Introduction, and Katharine Radice the commentary and vocabulary. Maps and the family tree are reprinted with thanks from N. P. Miller's excellent edition of Tacitus *Annals* I, and much of the material in this edition has been guided by her superb introduction and notes. Our thanks are due to Nicola Devlin and Dominic Rathbone for advice on the Introduction, to Stephen Anderson for his incisively accurate comments and observations on the first draft of the notes, to Bloomsbury's reviewer and to OCR's anonymous reader for their helpful suggestions, and to Alice Wright and her team at Bloomsbury Academic.

Katharine Radice
Roland Mayer
September 2015

Introduction

The historical situation

The extracts from Tacitus' *Annals* presented in this book focus on a specific moment in the history of Rome: the beginning of Tiberius' absolute control of the government of Rome in the year 14*. But Tacitus' readers, especially those in the senatorial elite, already knew a good deal about how the government of Rome came to be concentrated in the hands of one man, not least because they lived under just such a form of government. To understand why the accession of Tiberius was so significant, it will help to give a brief sketch both of the transition of government to its autocratic form and of some of the flaws integral to the nature of the principate.

Tacitus himself saw the need for just such a sketch and he provided it at the very beginning of the first book of the *Annals*. Rome was originally ruled by kings, the last of whom was expelled for tyrannical behaviour. Thus for ever after the word king, *rex*, and monarchical control were unacceptable in political life. In 509 BC what we call the republican form of government was adopted with the election of two consuls. The chief principles of this republican system were: collegiality – no individual had absolute power, which was shared among the annually elected magistrates; *libertas* – a fluid concept perhaps best rendered by 'political freedom'; and finally open debate – policy and legislation were to be discussed and decided by the free adult male citizenry. One institution survived from the days of the kings, namely the Senate. The Senate's function had been, and remained after the expulsion of the kings, advisory: senators held elective office and

---

* All dates are AD, unless otherwise designated.

commanded the armies, but as a body the Senate's formal role was to advise the magistrates, especially the two consuls. But as the Roman state grew in size, administration of its affairs – military, financial and legislative – became increasingly complex, so that the Senate and individual senators secured ever greater control of government business. This encouraged individual ambition, which tended to undermine the principle of collegiality. This was again something to which Tacitus drew particular attention in his preface to the *Annals*: in the first century BC the traditional system began to crumble under the power, supported by their prolonged command of loyal armies, of men like Cinna, Sulla and above all Pompey and Julius Caesar. The inevitable tensions among these 'warlords' produced a twenty-year-long period of civil wars, from 49 to 31 BC, which was ended only when Marcus Antonius was defeated at the battle of Actium by Octavian.

Octavian subsequently adopted the name Augustus and used the traditional but vague term *princeps*, 'first or chief citizen', to describe his non-elected position. We thus speak of this new form of government as the principate, borrowing Tacitus' own word, *principatus* (*Agricola* 3.1). As Tacitus noted when he used the word, there existed an incompatibility between the essentially monarchic position of the *princeps* and the older collegiate principle. This incompatibility was, however, masked by Augustus' claim to have 'restored' traditional power to the elected magistrates after the disorders of the prolonged civil wars. In effect this brings us to the situation found in the political life of Rome upon the death of Augustus. What followed was to determine the sort of world in which Tacitus and his readers found themselves. The succession of Tiberius established the principate as a dynasty, which lasted until the suicide of Nero in 68. There followed another period of widespread civil war as individuals jockeyed for position. Finally the general Vespasian established his own dynasty, the Flavian, which lasted until 96, when the cruel and autocratic Domitian was assassinated. Tacitus grew up and began his public career under Flavian rule. But he began his literary career only after the accession of a new emperor, Nerva, whose reign seemed to offer the hope that writers would be free to express their true thoughts about the past and the present.

Government by *princeps*

Augustus reigned for a long time, during which his control of the government and the administration as *princeps* was gradually developed, often with setbacks and readjustments. He is unlikely ever to have had a detailed plan of exactly what form the government of Rome should take. His own power, *imperium*, was based upon two things: first, possession of permanent tribunician power (*tribunicia potestas*); and second, his role as commander-in-chief of most of the legions and of his elite corps, the Praetorian Guard, which was stationed in Rome and attended upon the emperor and his family. In addition to his *imperium* he also enjoyed 'personal ascendancy', *auctoritas*, a concept difficult to pin down or define, but one of considerable importance in Roman social and political life. It is also clear that Augustus intended to keep power within his own family and to leave it to a successor as *princeps*; in short he wanted to found a ruling dynasty. The construction of a family mausoleum, remains of which can still be seen in Rome, was the visible and material expression of this aspiration. The difficulties he encountered in realizing this dynastic agenda are sketched by Tacitus and will be discussed below, but for now it will suffice to say that Tiberius had to be adopted as Augustus' son and designated as his heir. In this capacity Tiberius was groomed for the role he would one day assume; in the year 4 he became Augustus' 'colleague' and sharer in the tribunician power, as Tacitus noted at 3.3: *collega imperii, consors tribuniciae potestatis*. But since the concept of the *princeps* was entirely abstract (it wasn't an elected public office like the consulship), the 'principate' itself was not something that could be either bequeathed or inherited. This produces for us the paradox that on the death of Augustus, Tiberius both was and wasn't *princeps*. What Tacitus tries to describe in one of our extracts is how he eventually did become *princeps*.

Since our extracts focus on two important aspects of the imperial political system, namely the relation between the *princeps* and the Senate and his control of the army, it will be useful to offer a brief account about Augustus' policy and practice to provide more context for Tacitus' narrative of the succession debate and the mutinies.

One of the unlooked-for disadvantages of the principate was the diminished role of the Senate. The *princeps* was himself a senator and for practical purposes he needed the Senate, since administrators of provinces and commanders of armies were traditionally drawn from it. In the course of his long reign Augustus always aimed to maintain, and even to enhance, the prestige of the Senate and of senatorial families; to that end he reduced the Senate's number to about 600 and he cut down the annual number of administrative officials known as *quaestors*, thus checking fresh admissions to the body. Senators also now had to be, as we might say today, of 'high net worth'. Furthermore, Augustus set about comprehensively moulding the administrative role and procedure of the Senate, not in every respect to the liking of the senators (senators, like students, didn't like compulsory attendance). But what Augustus could not legislate for was his own position within the Senate. He found it most difficult to encourage the senators to speak their minds freely in his presence. Many factors contributed to this effective silencing of free speech, and the silencing itself marginalized the Senate as an advisory body. Senators knew that policy was formulated by the *princeps* in consultation either with his group of friends and advisors, later called the *consilium*, or with the small senatorial 'executive committee' which he had formed in 18 BC, so that open, independent debate seemed pointless once the matter was laid before the Senate itself. (Tiberius did away with this committee.) By the time of Augustus' death therefore it is hardly surprising that the senators assumed that Tiberius' accession was what we might call a 'done deal', and discussion of it would serve no purpose except to alienate the new ruler of Rome. The serious problem for the senators was not so much the accession itself as the lack of a clear procedure for validating it.

For the army too Augustus passed measures designed to turn the legions into permanent units and to make military service a career for volunteers. He therefore addressed such issues as length of service, *stipendium* ('pay'), and *praemia* ('rewards') upon discharge, thereby ensuring that the army looked to the *princeps* and to no one else as its sole benefactor. In 13 BC Augustus fixed the term of army service at sixteen years plus four in reserve; he also offered troops a cash 'reward' (*praemium*) upon discharge instead of allotting them property to farm (public land in Italy was becoming scarce). But in 5 the term of service was extended to twenty years with an additional five in reserve; there seems also to have been an increase in the cash reward. The problem for the emperor was honouring these commitments: how was he to pay the huge number of men serving under arms? This is not the place to go into Augustus' measures to ensure that there would be enough money to pay the soldiers' wages and then provide their pecuniary reward upon discharge. Suffice it to say that quelling the revolt in Pannonia between 6 and 9 and the loss of three legions in Germany in 9 had put severe strains on financing the troops. The death of Augustus produced just enough uncertainty to tip some of the legions into revolt with a view to securing from the new *princeps* redress of their grievances (16.1).

Other features of the Julio-Claudian principate deserve brief mention. As was suggested above the principate was effectively monarchic in character, even though the word *rex* was carefully avoided. All monarchs attract courtiers, and the *princeps* was no different. So the principate gave scope to non-senators to secure positions of influence within the imperial household (like Maecenas under Augustus). We encounter in our extracts two such figures, Sallustius Crispus (3.3) and Sejanus (1.24). Dynastic rule gave women and adoption much greater scope than ever before. Considering the fundamental role of the family in Roman life, marriage and the production of a male heir had always been important. But traditionally adoption had been a last resort for men without sons and marriage could cement political alliances; for instance Pompey married Julius Caesar's daughter, and Octavian's sister married Marcus Antonius. But under the early principate both marriage and adoption came to underpin the dynastic principle. For example, in 12 BC Tiberius was made to divorce his wife Vipsania and marry Augustus' daughter, the immoral Julia, a marriage that brought him closer to the *princeps*. Much later the young Nero would be married to Octavia, the daughter of Claudius; in due course he would be brought legally into the family by adoption (weirdly, this entailed Octavia's adoption into another family so that she wouldn't be married to her 'brother'!). By the same token women, as wives and mothers, acquired enhanced influence (but never actual power, which only men could wield). Augustus' wife Livia, the mother of Tiberius, was the first imperial woman to exercise considerable control; Tacitus notes in one of our extracts how she openly lobbied for her son's advancement (3.3). Nero's mother, the

THE JULIO-CLAUDIANS

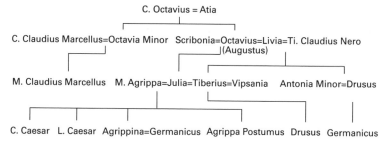

Figure 1.1 The Julio-Claudian family.

younger Agrippina, would prove a very adroit manipulator of men and of events. The role of these high-bred ladies is perhaps one of the fascinations for Tacitus of the Julio-Claudian reigns; certainly the Flavian dynasty did much to control their womenfolk, but then the Flavian succession didn't depend on adoption.

Historical sources

None of the sources upon which Tacitus himself relied for information has survived. From Velleius Paterculus, who was a soldier and senator under Tiberius, we do have a brief history of the period, but it does not seem that Tacitus made any use of it, perhaps because Velleius strongly approved of Tiberius. Although Tacitus consulted chiefly his historiographical predecessors, he also seems to have read formal edicts, speeches and letters, as well as autobiographies and biographies. There were also official reports of senatorial business which he may have used.

We have two main sources of information for this period in addition to Tacitus. First, there are the imperial biographies of his younger contemporary, Suetonius; of equestrian rank, he was an imperial administrator and so had access to the archival material of the *principes*. Second, there is the third-century historian, Cassius Dio; he was an ethnic Greek, and so wrote in Greek, but he was also, like Tacitus, a Roman senator. He used the sources Tacitus used, but doesn't seem to have used Tacitus (he may have found his Latin too difficult).

The accession of Tiberius

Augustus died on 19 August 14, after controlling the Roman world since 27 BC as *princeps*. Like any other elite Roman male, when contemplating the prospect of his own death, he drew up a will in which he would bequeath a portion of his personal estate to his eldest son. Fate had refused him a biological son, but Roman law remedied this defect by permitting adoption. So Augustus adopted, naturally within his own family. But once again Fate was unkind and all the candidates for heir from within the Julian family predeceased him. (All but one, to be precise, but Agrippa Postumus was for various reasons totally unthinkable, and had been banished to an island (3.4).) So Augustus had to look outside his own bloodline for an heir. He didn't have to look far since his wife, Livia, had two sons by her first husband, and Augustus adopted the elder, Tiberius (3.3).

Augustus intended to leave his heir something more than a share of his personal estate. He envisaged his family as the dynastic rulers of Rome, but there was no precedent for the testamentary bequest of political power. The succession of Augustus was therefore to be an innovation in Rome's political system. If his private-law heir somehow became the next *princeps* then the principle of hereditary succession to the principate would be effectively established. On the other hand, there was an alternative: a new *princeps* might be chosen from within the senatorial elite by the Senate itself. So in adopting Tiberius, Augustus clearly intended that he should succeed both to his personal estate and to control of the government of the empire.

Tiberius was in theory a sound choice. Born in 42 BC into the less distinguished of the two Claudian families, he had been early advanced into the Senate. He enjoyed diplomatic and military successes as a young man; Horace celebrated his achievements in a late ode, 4.4. Tiberius' impressive career in the army would readily secure him the loyalty of the legions and of the Praetorian Guard. Where his position was arguably less satisfactory was in the Senate, and paradoxically it was his military service that might have unfitted him to deal with his fellow senators. Much of his time had either been spent on campaign or in self-imposed seclusion on the island of Rhodes, where he had lived in retirement for eight years until his return to Rome in 2. He thus hadn't mastered the means of managing his fellow senators by forging personal alliances and friendships within that body. Military command may also have deprived him of tact: he was used to commanding, not to persuading. His aristocratic pride, noted by Tacitus at 4.3, *insita Claudiae familiae superbia*, probably didn't help him a lot either. On his adoption in 4 he had been granted the crucial tribunician power for ten years, which was renewed for a further ten in 13, and he also held proconsular *imperium*, so that he was effectively in full power on the death of Augustus. Nonetheless his accession, which is where Tacitus begins his *Annals*, was not as trouble-free as might have been hoped.

Tacitus briskly makes clear the background (Chapters 3–7). He sketches the problems Augustus had had to surmount in securing a suitable heir in Chapter 3. On Augustus' death he notes that Tiberius took command of the army, by giving the watchword to the Praetorian Guard and by communicating with the legions in the provinces (Chapter 7). Hesitation, however, arose when he faced the Senate; Tiberius wanted to give his succession to full political control the validation of its support. But such a personal transfer of power was, as noted above, unprecedented, so there was no procedure to be followed for validation. Tiberius showed no skill in negotiating this difficulty, and Tacitus dwells on the confused and confusing meeting of the Senate on 17 September 14 (Chapters 11–14), when Tiberius' position as *princeps* was somehow or other acknowledged and the principle of dynastic succession established.

Awkward as dealing with the Senate proved, it posed no threat to the very institution of the principate, or, more specifically, the position of Tiberius. That threat came from the army, and almost immediately Tiberius had to deal with mutinies in Pannonia and in Germany. Considerable narrative space in the first book of the *Annals* is given to these mutinies and their settlement because the relation between the *princeps* and his armies will be of crucial importance throughout the period covered by the *Annals*, up to the death of Nero – who took fright and committed suicide when a revolt of the army in Upper Germany was reported in 68. So these initial mutinies highlight a fundamental theme of the subsequent narrative. The account of the Pannonian mutiny (Chapters 16–30) also allows the reader to compare the behaviour of Tiberius' sons Drusus and the adopted Germanicus, who dealt with the legionary uprising in Germany (Chapters 31–45 in English, and 46–49 in Latin).

Historiography at Rome

Fabius Pictor, the earliest prose historian of Rome, wrote in Greek, partly because he aimed to insert himself into the long and distinguished tradition of Greek historiography, and partly to make the national story palatable to an international readership; in the Mediterranean basin more people spoke and read Greek than Latin when he wrote the first Roman history in the late third century BC. Over time, however, national sentiment and the enhanced flexibility of the Latin language encouraged the use of Latin for history. Nonetheless there was for a long time something of a problem in devising an appropriate literary style for historiography, a matter that will be dealt with below.

Roman historians owed much to the Greek tradition. Perhaps the most conspicuous formal feature derived from the Greeks is the insertion of speeches, both direct and reported, into the narrative, something unthinkable nowadays, unless the actual words were certainly recorded. But oratory was such an important feature of public life in the ancient world that formal speeches could hardly be omitted from the historical record. This had something of a knock-on effect upon the historians themselves, and later Greek and most Roman historiography is heavily influenced by rhetoric, the systematized art of persuasion.

On the other hand, from the earliest period Roman historical writing had certain features peculiar to itself. Most significantly, it was generally written by senators, the men who held the magistracies, who led the armies and who governed the provinces. (Tacitus' chief model, Sallust, was a senator; the exception to this 'rule' was the great Augustan historian, Livy.) Senators were in the best position to understand and explain the course of events, in which they might themselves have taken part (it should be remembered that most 'ancient' historians wrote about contemporary events, not the remote past). But they were also limited in their outlook: Rome, its government and the Senate were the focus of their attention. Nor were they always disinterested: in an historical narrative scores could be settled, or family achievements magnified. Over time, however, political and military activity fell more and more under the control of a small number of powerful individuals, who necessarily came to dominate the historical record. With the change of political system under Augustus the character of the ruler became a dominant factor in events, and the historian had to be something of a biographer and psychologist as well.

Some (but by no means all) Roman historians used a characteristic framework for their narrative, an annual organization of events in chronological order. For this reason such narratives are sometimes called *annales*, derived from *annus* ('year'). Sallust's major work, despite its title *Historiae*, was composed annalistically. Livy and Tacitus also adopted this framework (the first change of year in Tacitus' *Annales* comes at Chapter 55).

Another feature of Roman historiography was the strength of its moralizing strain. A moralistic element served to justify many forms of literature at Rome: reading wasn't an idle pastime, but provided moral improvement and inspiration. This was especially true of the accounts of the national experience, as a number of historians, most notably Livy, pointed out. The historian performed a public service not just by recording the past as truthfully as possible, but by holding up exemplary figures for imitation or, in the case of villains, for condemnation. This has rightly been described as the task of self-definition; the historian above all was in a position to give an account of what it was like to be a Roman.

Tacitus

Cornelius Tacitus, whose *praenomen* ('first name') is still uncertain, was born in the second half of the 50s, early in Nero's reign. We do not know where he was born. His father or possibly uncle may have been a Cornelius Tacitus mentioned by the elder Pliny, *Natural History* 7.76, as an imperial civil administrator (*procurator*) in the province of Gallia Belgica (nowadays Northern France, roughly). If so, his father was an equestrian, and his son can be seen to embark upon the career of a *nouus homo* ('new man') by seeking entry to the Senate and high office. A *procurator* was well paid and could afford the sort of further education that would equip his son for social and political advancement. The chief study of any young Roman who aimed to rise, assuming he lacked strong military aspirations, was rhetoric, since rhetorical training prepared him to speak both in the law courts – where dazzling reputations could be made – and in the Senate. Tacitus presumably trained in Rome, where in the reign of Vespasian he attached himself to an eminent barrister, Marcus Aper, who is mentioned in one of his early works, the *Dialogus de oratoribus*.

In the introduction to his first historical work, the so-called *Historiae*, Tacitus told his readers, without specifying his age or providing dates, that his public career was initiated by the emperor Vespasian: *dignitatem nostram a Vespasiano inchoatam* (1.1.3). This may mean that the emperor allowed him to wear on his tunic, the garment worn beneath the toga, a broad purple stripe (*latus clauus*).

This imperial favour (*beneficium*) was bestowed on quite young men – they might still be in their mid-teens – who were seen to be on the way up; success as pleaders in the law courts guaranteed visibility. Once Tacitus was marked out in this way, further promotions were on the cards. Additional information may now be provided by an inscription, long neglected, that has recently been reinvestigated and identified cautiously as the epitaph of the historian.

The stone records that the honorand was a member of the panel of ten for deciding disputes (*decemuir stlitibus iudicandis*). To put this into context: young men with prospects of entering the Senate were appointed to the so-called *vigintivirate*, a set of four minor magistracies that marked another step up. One of these magistracies was open only to the sons of senators, so it is significant that the honorand was in the one of the remaining three which conferred the greatest prestige. By his late teens or early twenties Tacitus would be at least considering two career moves, in the form of appointment as a military tribune and marriage respectively. He married the daughter of Gnaeus Julius Agricola, during or just after Agricola's consulship in 76/77 (*Agr.* 9.6). He was now on the threshold of his senatorial career.

At about the age of twenty-five, a Roman could hold his first important magistracy, the quaestorship: important, because it gave admission to the Senate. The epitaph mentioned above records that the honorand, like Pliny, had a special sort of quaestorship, since he was designated 'quaestor Augusti'. The *princeps'* quaestor was, obviously, his personal choice, and his main function was to read out the communications of the *princeps* to the Senate. Such a man was clearly being singled out for high office. It is also worth noting the value such a post could have for a future historian. Reading letters was not the whole of his job; the *princeps'* personal quaestor must have been closely involved in imperial business: for instance, Tiberius' quaestor, Aulus Plautius, wrote out with his own hand the Senate's decree in the trial of Calpurnius Piso. In short, this quaestorship gave its holder an unprecedented insight into the secret workings of imperial policy and administration.

Whether or not the inscription describes the career of Tacitus, we can be confident that he was by now well launched. He was praetor in 88, under Domitian, as he tells us himself in *Ann.* 11.11, a passage in which he mentions something else about his social, rather than political, standing: he had by that time been appointed to one of the four priestly *collegia* or 'boards of officials', the fifteen men who supervised foreign cults and looked after the prophetic Sibylline books (*quindecimuiri sacris faciundis*). Assuming he was now about thirty years of age, this was an impressive marker of his social rise, since 'new men' usually had to wait until after their consulship to find themselves in one of these 'colleges'. We now meet with a gap in his career, but it is likely that after the praetorship he served as the legate of a legion for three years and as a provincial governor for one. At any rate it is clear from what he says at *Agricola* 45.4–45.5 that he was away from Rome for a period of four years, from 89 to 93.

The Rome to which Tacitus returned was terrorized by the increasingly autocratic Domitian. Tacitus himself sketches the appalling situation for the Senate in the closing pages of *Agricola*, 44.5–45.2. And yet Tacitus' own rise was unhindered, and he was appointed suffect, i.e., replacement, consul in the latter part of 97, a year or so before the typical age of forty-three; Domitian probably selected him for the promotion. It was within a year or so of Domitian's assassination, in September of 96, that Tacitus commenced his career as a writer of something other than speeches for court or Senate, with the publication of his biography of his late father-in-law, Agricola. He continued to be active in public life. In 100 he, along with Pliny, was entrusted by the Senate with the prosecution of a rapacious provincial governor, Marius Priscus, and thanks to yet another inscription we know that in about 112–113 he secured the crown of a senatorial career, the proconsulship of the peaceful and luxurious Roman province of Asia (now the Aegean seaboard of Turkey, more or less). There is no evidence for the time of his death.

Tacitus' social and political career is fundamental to an appreciation of his literary work. Two of his early works, the biography of Agricola and the dialogue on orators, are the fruits of his own experience, as Agricola's son-in-law and as Rome's leading orator both in courts and in the Senate. If he was a *quaestor Augusti* then he had a privileged insight into the workings of autocracy, which would have been of inestimable value to an historian. But another reason for sketching an ancient historian's life is the issue of his authority. Tacitus' career endowed his historical writing with the authority of a senator. In the prefatory remarks to his *Historiae*, 1.1.1, he complains that truth, the historian's goal, was diminished after the battle of Actium (31 BC) and the establishment of the principate by, among other things, an ignorance of public policy (*inscitia rei publicae*). As a senator of the highest standing, Tacitus could claim a measure of the understanding required for a balanced and accurate account of the past. So his career is a sort of guarantee of authority. We may now turn to his career as an historian.

After the removal of Domitian, Tacitus felt the freshening breeze of literary revival mentioned by Pliny in the first of his published letters. He followed his biography of Agricola, at no long interval, with an ethnographical survey of Germany. Finally by way of literary debut, he wrote the *Dialogus*, an exchange of views on the state of contemporary oratory. Its publication date is uncertain, but many feel that the year 102, in which the dedicatee Fabius Justus was consul, is satisfactory. The first two works can be seen as preparatory to the writing of history, since the biography contains ethnographical and narrative passages, and even the traditional contrasting speeches delivered by generals before battle. We infer from some later letters of Pliny that by about 106 Tacitus was composing his first full-scale historiographical work, the *Histories* (*Epistles* 6.16, 7.20 and 33, and 8.7), the books of which may have been published serially, rather than all at the same time. The period covered in this work started with the reign of Galba in 68 and closed with the assassination of Domitian; in other words, it comprised the whole of the Flavian dynasty. Sometime after he completed the *Histories* he began the *Annals*, later in the reign of Trajan (98–117). How long it took him to compose, or if he even lived long enough to finish the work, is not known.

The *Annals*

Tacitus did not entitle this work *Annales*; that title is owed to a sixteenth-century editor of the text, Vetranius. The original title was probably *Ab Excessu Divi Augusti* ('From the Death of the Deified Augustus'), similar to the title of Livy's history of Rome, *Ab Urbe Condita* ('From the Foundation of the City'). The year-by-year annalistic narrative covered the fifty-four-year period from the death of Augustus and the accession of Tiberius to the death of Nero. At any rate it is reckoned that Nero's suicide, which brought to an end the Julio-Claudian dynasty, was the envisaged conclusion, whether or not the historian lived to narrate it. Why Tacitus chose to move back in time for his second work of history is a question variously answered.

He says in his prefatory remarks to the work that the rise of flattery under autocratic rule scared off serious talent. He further claims that during the reigns of Augustus' successors fear produced false accounts in their lifetimes or, once they were dead, the bias of loathing. Since Tacitus didn't live under their rule he brought neither anger nor partiality to the account. In short, he reckoned that he was in a position to strike a necessary balance in telling the story of the Julio-Claudian *principes*. But there may be an additional reason for going so far back in time. It was suggested above that one of the characteristic features of Roman historiography was the issue of self-identity, accounting for what it is like to be a Roman, but not an everyday Roman-in-thestreet of course, rather a Roman of the senatorial elite, the class of person who even under the principate still played an important part in government and the administration of the territorial empire, and who wrote up the history of the period. In going back to the reign of the first imperial successor, Tacitus seems to be looking for the factors which shaped his own world. Arguably he identified the chief factor in the dynastic succession itself. Let us see how he suggests that.

After the burial of Augustus, the senators met to consider Tiberius' role (Chapter 11) and it is made clear that they were eager for him to shoulder the burden alone, despite his own apparent, and presumably unexpected, reluctance. In the debate which followed (Chapters 12–13) two named senators, Asinius Gallus and Lucius Arruntius, posed questions to Tiberius which he had not foreseen and so had difficulty answering: this gave offence (a common problem in the principate, as we see in the letters of the younger Pliny). Since these senators make their first appearance here in the narrative, Tacitus tells us something about Tiberius' attitude to them: he was already hostile to Gallus (12.4) and suspicious of Arruntius (13.1). Then, surprisingly, Tacitus puts the brakes on the forward movement of the narrative. Students of narrative technique, narratologists, would recognize in 13.2–13.3 a device they call analepsis, a moving back to an earlier time to pick up some information not related in its proper chronological place. Tacitus makes it clear that he is moving back in time to one of Augustus' last conversations (*supremis sermonibus*) in which he canvassed possible rival claimants to the principate; Gallus and Arruntius turn out to be two of the men he thought might be prepared to assume the role of *princeps*. Tacitus thus implies that the succession, even in Augustus' eyes, did not have to be dynastic, since there were alternatives outside his own family. Tiberius had indeed been groomed for the job, but if a suitable rival opposed him, and presumably secured the Senate's support, then the succession became an open issue ever after. What happened at this crucial debate, however, was that the Senate accepted the dynastic principle and so dug its own grave. The Senate committed its support to the heir of the previous *princeps* and so forfeited a measure of freedom. This debate was decisive for the shaping of the role and character of the Senate right down to the time of Tacitus himself, whose career had advanced under a subsequent dynasty, the Flavian. So his choice to begin the *Annals* with the death of Augustus and the accession of Tiberius seems exactly right, if the personal issue for the historian was to explain how his own world came to be the way it was. Before leaving this episode of the story it is worth pointing out that Chapter 13 contains not only a narrative analepsis, but also a prolepsis – or anticipation of events – at 13.3, where Tacitus observes, rather inaccurately, that all the men whom Augustus had identified as possible claimants of the principate (with the exception of the unambitious Lepidus) were in due course overthrown by Tiberius.

Another reason for starting the narrative of the *Annals* with the accession of Tiberius is that Tacitus pretty clearly saw the last member of the Julio-Claudian line, Nero, as a kind of deformed echo of Augustus' first successor. For instance, both men were adopted into the Julian family and came to the purple through the scheming of their mothers, Livia and Agrippina; these women enjoyed high influence in the early years of their sons' reigns, even to the extent of doing away with potential rivals, Agrippa Postumus and Junius Silanus, without the knowledge of their sons. The reigns of both emperors started reasonably well, but both men in due course fell under the influence of malignant prefects of the Praetorian Guard, Sejanus and Tigellinus, who encouraged them in scandalously self-indulgent lifestyles. So there was a sort of tidy circularity in the story of Augustus' successors which had an artistic appeal to the historian.

We may now look more closely at the extracts which illustrate Augustus' efforts to ensure the succession, the problems of dealing with the Senate and of managing the discontents of the army.

The succession (Chapters 3–7)

After the brief introductory paragraphs, Tacitus sets out in some detail the problems Augustus had in securing a successor. Naturally he wanted someone who shared his own blood, so he nominated first his sister's son Marcellus, and then the sons of Agrippa by his daughter Julia. Inconveniently, however, they all died (3.3). Tacitus seizes the opportunity to mention, but not repudiate, the belief that Augustus' wife Livia had a hand in the deaths of Gaius and Lucius, presumably so as to promote the prospects of her remaining son Tiberius. (Such a scenario also serves as a pre-echo of the schemes of Agrippina to advance her son Nero under Claudius, which Tacitus will relate later on.) Tiberius survived, and became full partner in control of the state. The section ends, however, with a glance at a possible rival, Augustus' uncouth grandson Agrippa Postumus (3.4) and with the addition of a further prop to the succession: even though he has a son of his own, Drusus, Tiberius is made to adopt his nephew Germanicus, who is given an important command. Tacitus is, as it were, setting out the pieces on a chessboard: we will soon learn of the murder of Postumus (Chapters 5–6) and Tiberius' two sons will figure in accounts of the mutinies.

With the succession issue cleared up, Tacitus glances at the state of the empire: beyond Rome only Germany gives cause for alarm (3.6; again, we are told this to prepare for the mutiny), within Rome itself all is calm (3.7). Tacitus turns now to the political situation in the city towards the end of Augustus' life (Chapter 4). Few knew what it was like to live with complete political freedom and so most accepted the rule of one man, though alternatives—a return to political freedom, civil war—were possibilities (4.2). But most men felt that power would come into the hands of just one man, but which man was it to be after Augustus' death, given that one blood relation survived, Postumus? Tacitus describes their reflections dramatically, as if two opposed parties were exchanging views (4.3–4.4, all in indirect discourse). The crucial considerations are left to the end of the section (4.5): Livia will continue to be a force to be reckoned with if Tiberius succeeds, and now that he has two sons, their rivalry for succession (Tiberius was fifty-six) will surely prove problematic.

Tacitus has thus placed all his pieces on the chessboard and it is now time to set them in motion. Augustus is ailing (was Livia behind this too?) and there was a rumour that he visited his exiled grandson (5.1–5.2). Reporting rumour is an important feature of Tacitean narrative, because the existence of a rumour is itself a fact, even if its content is untrue. A rumour may be believed by many and recorded by an historian, who serves as a source. So rumour does matter, however baseless it may be. Another feature of Tacitean narrative deserves note in this paragraph: uncertainty. Twice the historian admits that he doesn't know what actually happened: did Fabius Maximus commit suicide (5.2), was Augustus dead or alive when Tiberius returned to him at Nola (5.3)? Paradoxically, the frank admission of uncertainty guarantees the historian's reliability when he states facts as facts; if he is honest enough to admit what he doesn't know, then he must be confident in recording what he does know. In addition Tacitus hints at why facts are hard to establish under autocracy: much business is conducted in secret. Livia (again!) had barricaded the villa in which Augustus died so all anyone knew, after the cheerful bulletins, was that he was dead and Tiberius was in charge (5.4).

The new reign begins with a judicial murder in Chapter 6 (again, a pre-echo of the reign of Nero, compare *Annals* 13.1). Tacitus' problem is once again the secrecy shrouding autocracy: who ordered the death of Agrippa Postumus? Tacitus pretty clearly believes Tiberius was implicated, but modern historians reckon that yet again it was Livia who ordered the killing, with the connivance of Sallustius Crispus. The issue of fact must be left unresolved, but the crucial point of the episode seems to be the very last sentence of the section, since it contains, in epigrammatic form, an observation about government by one man: accounts only balance if submitted to the approval of one person alone. This observation undermines Tiberius' notion that he should provide an 'account' of the death for the Senate. Crispus, the shrewd 'civil servant', knows this won't work. By recording his remark Tacitus gives the reader an insight into one of the fundamental principles of autocracy, a principle Tiberius needs to learn.

With a rival out of the way, Tacitus turns to the reception of Augustus' successor and his first summoning of the Senate as *princeps*. The mass of men are eager to prolong their 'enslavement' (*servitium* 7.1). The keynote here is pretence: not only are the senators disingenuous (*falsi* 7.1), Tiberius himself conceals his real feelings and intentions, at any rate according to Tacitus (*inductam dubitationem* 7.7), whose point is that members of the senatorial elite no longer deal with each other as equals who speak their minds plainly. Modern historians feel that he is probably being unfair to Tiberius, whose hesitation, faithfully recorded here by Tacitus (*ambiguus imperandi* 7.3), may well have been genuine. In this section Tacitus also alleges Tiberius' suspicion of Germanicus (7.6), which is again something modern historians are reluctant to credit.

The debate about succession in the Senate (Chapters 11–14)

After his burial, the divine status of Augustus was formally recognized by the Senate on 17 September 14 with the establishment of his cult (*templum et caelestes religiones decernuntur* 10.8). The next issue (*inde* 11.1) was the role of Tiberius, presumably defined for senatorial approval in a *relatio*, 'motion', of the presiding consul. But it is odd that not one of our sources gives precise information on the terms of that motion. At any rate, if normal procedure was followed the motion would next be debated and amendments could be suggested by senators, who were called upon to speak in order of seniority after the consuls designate. After debate a vote might be taken, and if positive its result was embodied in a *senatus consultum*, 'decree of the Senate'. In the present case, the apparently free choice of the Senate would secure Tiberius' position as *princeps*, and incidentally establish the dynastic principle of succession in Rome. Tacitus, who provides our most complete account of the debate, does not however describe it along the lines of procedure just sketched. He chose an altogether more dramatically vivid and impressionistic story line.

Tacitus begins, not with the consular motion, but with the prayers of the senators. There may be a calculated irony in the expression *versae . . . ad Tiberium preces*, which follows immediately upon the apotheosis of Augustus: Tiberius is the real object of prayer, not the now deified Augustus. Tacitus doesn't mention the consular motion, but describes what must be taken to be Tiberius' reaction to it, a reluctance to take up the burden of government all on his own. Tacitus puts into his mouth as one reason for this reluctance the quality of diffidence, *modestia*. This word, along with others of similar sense, such as *pudor* at 12.2, is going to prove important in the historian's characterization of the new *princeps*. Other sources confirm that Tiberius had misgivings about his ability to rule without support. At 11.3 the highly emotional response of the senators to this show of reluctance is described. To convince them of the difficulties of sole rule, Tiberius produces a document of Augustus', outlining the massive scale of imperial administration. This seems designed to convince the Senate that the job could not realistically be managed by one man alone. Again, the Senate's grovelling reaction is recorded (*infimas obtestationes* 12.2), which elicits from Tiberius a chance remark (*dixit forte*). We now see what Tacitus is up to: he is describing a situation in which no one has a really clear game plan: everyone – Tiberius, the senators – is making it up as they go along, each taking a sort of cue from what happens before, what nowadays we might call an 'omnishambles'. By way of response to that chance remark, Asinius Gallus asks Tiberius a question, a question for which Tacitus makes it clear that Tiberius was totally unprepared and didn't know how to reply (*perculsus improvisa interrogatione paulum reticuit* 12.2): no practised politician is ever caught 'on the back foot'. Tiberius still wanted to get the senators to make a clear proposal for power-sharing, and Gallus, realizing he had blundered, tried to patch things up, unsuccessfully. What follows in Tacitus' account has already been discussed above, the strange flashback in Chapter 13 to Augustus' assessment of possible rivals for the imperial purple. At 13.4–13.5 the forward narrative resumes, and matters are finally brought to some sort of resolution after the intervention of two more blundering senators: it isn't that Tiberius expressly agreed to the consular motion, the existence of which Tacitus at this late point in the story gets round to mentioning, but he stopped saying no (*negare … desineret*). Once that crucial point had been carried, some further business is described in Chapter 14.

Tacitus' account of the discussion is designed to highlight its random character: there is no hint of plan or design in anyone's mind and Tiberius seems to have launched a grenade by proposing to share the control the Senate was prepared to entrust to him, a control for which Augustus had been preparing him. Most modern assessments of Tacitus' account chiefly find fault with his assurance that both Tiberius and the Senate were insincere during this debate. He regarded Tiberius' expression of diffidence as dishonest: 11.2 *plus in oratione tali dignitatis quam fidei erat*, a view endorsed by Suetonius, *Tiberius* Chapter 24, who called it a charade. The Senate is reckoned equally disingenuous: 11.3 *unus metus si intellegere viderentur*. This conviction of complicity in pretence colours his whole account of this debate. But for some time now historians have challenged this interpretation, mainly as being a retrojection of the sort of hypocrisy that Tacitus himself was used to back to a time when it had yet to come into operation. We can never know why Tiberius came so unprepared to that senatorial debate. He wanted the Senate's validation of his position and he ought to have anticipated the terms of the consular motion, which must have reflected Augustus' intentions. It would also have helped to have prepared some senators to support his scheme for power-sharing, assuming it was both genuine and at all feasible. But clearly the whole business was conducted in a fog of misunderstanding. Tacitus for his part did not credit the possibility of mutual misunderstanding, and assumed that the Tiberian Senate was as hypocritical as the Domitianic.

The Pannonian mutiny (Chapters 16–30)

The territory known to the Romans as Pannonia (see Figure 1.2) nowadays comprises western Hungary. It had been the scene of much campaigning since the late Republic, but it had not been subdued and reduced to the status of a province. Between 6 and 9 the peoples of Pannonia and nearby Illyricum revolted against Rome and for three years fought a vigorous war which Suetonius regarded as the most dangerous to Rome since Hannibal (*Tiberius* Chapter 16). It was chiefly Tiberius who ended this war successfully for Rome; he celebrated a triumph in 10. But the cost to the state of the extraordinary levies and of remobilizing veterans must have been considerable. Moreover the loss of three legions under Quinctilius Varus in Germany in 9 put further strain on military resources. Money was clearly scarce and so instead of the cash payment of the 'reward' on discharge, land – but of poor quality and not in Italy – was being awarded to the troops who had completed their terms of service. This is a particular grievance mentioned among the others – prolonged service, low pay, corrupt centurions – by the rabble-rouser Percennius (17.3). The death of Augustus, to whom the troops had sworn

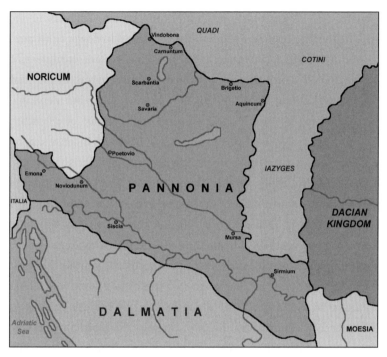

Figure 1.2 Pannonia at the time of the military revolt Tacitus records in Chapter 16ff.

allegiance, seemed to provide them with the opportunity to put pressure on his successor for redress.

The troops in Pannonia were the first to mutiny and they were followed by those in Germany. Tiberius sent his own son Drusus to deal with the former (Chapter 24); his adoptive son Germanicus, who had been conducting a census in Gaul when Augustus' death was announced, went to Germany. Accompanying Drusus was the immensely influential prefect of the Praetorian Guard, Aelius Sejanus; though he had nothing to do with settling the mutiny, the opportunity of introducing him into the story at an early stage and thus paving the way for his later prominence – another example of narrative prolepsis – was not to be missed. Our extracts cover the whole of the Pannonian mutiny,

Chapters 16–30, and only a portion of the German, Chapters 46–49, relating the suppression of the revolt of the troops in Lower Germany.

Mutiny offered Tacitus material for varied and versatile treatment, of which 24.3–25.2 provide a fine example. There is contrast of pictorial details: no gleaming decorations but filth, faces not happy but menacing, fierce shouting followed by sudden quiet, and contrast of character: Drusus apparently unruffled and in control, the troops inconsistent, by turns aggressive or fearful. So we not only see and hear what is happening, a literary device which Roman critics called *evidentia* 'vividness', the mood-swings and emotions of the soldiers are also described.

Description is Tacitus' strong suit, but there is surprisingly little uninterrupted narrative. His account is in the strictest sense of the word dramatic: speech, both direct and reported, dominates the story. After the scene is set in Chapter 16, Percennius takes over with a long harangue in direct speech in which he lists the soldiers' grievances (Chapter 17). Though what follows (Chapter 18) is strictly speaking descriptive of the soldiers' response to the individual points raised by Percennius (their wounds, scars, white hair, shabby clothes and naked bodies), Tacitus makes it clear that they are shouting their support: *adstrepebat* (the narrative imperfect at the beginning of sentences should be noted too: 19.1 *aggerebatur*, 23.1 *incendebat*, 25.2 *stabat*, 30.3 *durabat*), *exprobrantes*. Then the legate Blaesus appears, shouting (*clamitans*). Once he has their attention he addresses them (Chapter 19), and the soldiers shout back at him (*adclamavere*). The scene then shifts to a company of sappers, and we hear their taunting of a hated camp superintendent (20.1 *rogitantes*). There is more shouting and insults and oaths as the mutineers are hauled off to jail (21.2). Then Vibulenus, lifted up on the mens' shoulders, appeals in direct speech to Blaesus (Chapter 22); afterwards he grovels at his comrades' feet (23.1). Once Drusus arrives on the scene there are more dramatic exchanges: he reads Tiberius' letter (25.3), and the troops respond (26.1). Drusus tries to reply but is shouted down, with the objections to his proposal set out by the angry soldiers. When Lentulus tries to leave the camp, we hear the insistent questions (27.2 *rogitantes*) hurled at him by the troops. The following sections are no different: there is some straightforward narrative but the action is really carried forward by what people are saying or thinking as the moon goes into eclipse.

One curiosity of this extended use of speech not just to animate but to constitute the narrative is the historian's critique of the quality of the main speakers: Percennius is *procax lingua*, Junius Blaesus is characterized by *multa dicendi arte*, but Drusus is *rudis dicendi*. Tacitus reveals his hand as himself an accomplished orator and critic of oratory. Another peculiarly Tacitean strategy is found at 19.5 where the troops are said to be proud of securing the legate's son as their ambassador. This is unlikely to have been part of the historical tradition, but Tacitus likes to expose the imagined thinking or motivation of the actors in his drama.

Even where we find straightforward narration Tacitus makes it especially memorable by focusing on the fate of an individual, at 20.1 Aufidienus Rufus, at 23.3 the centurion Lucilius (and we are even told his grim nickname, 'gimme another'), and at 27.2 Lentulus.

For the most part the narrative of the Pannonian mutiny is coherent, but one incoherence may be noted: Blaesus' son is sent to Rome at 19.4–19.5, but he is somehow or other again sent to Rome at 29.2. How did this come about? Did he meet Drusus on the way after his first departure and return with him to the camp? Tacitus clearly isn't interested in accounting for this detail.

The mutiny in Lower Germany
(Chapters 31–45 and 46–49)

Tacitus' account of the mutiny in the armies in Upper and Lower Germany (see Figure 1.3) is extensive. It is made clear at once, in Chapter 31, that of the two mutinies the German is the more threatening,

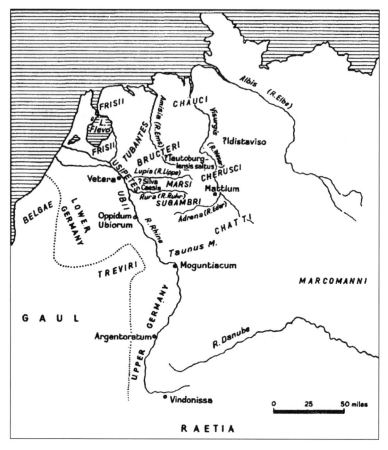

Figure 1.3 Germany showing the area of mutiny Tacitus records in Chapter 31ff.

first because of its extent and second because there is, Tacitus alleges, a hope that Germanicus will topple Tiberius (the reader has been prepared for this notion at 7.7, and why such a hope might have existed will be explained in Chapter 33). Tacitus then shows that the situation was different in the two sectors (Chapter 32), with the troops in Lower Germany leading the way. It is noted that unlike in Pannonia there were no ringleaders, evidence that the discontent was widespread and deep rooted. The scene describing Germanicus' arrival at the seditious camp and the soldiers' gross response to his appeals shows all the brilliance of Tacitus' descriptive skills (Chapters 34–35). The danger is so great that Germanicus and his advisors adopt an incompetent strategy, forging a letter as if from Tiberius (Chapter 36). The soldiers, seeing through the ruse, demand and secure instant satisfaction (Chapter 37). Their apparent success seems short-lived, however, on the arrival of an embassy from Rome, which it was thought would rescind the grants (Chapter 39); again, the vividness of the narrative, with a Roman ex-consul clinging for dear life to the eagle standard, is unequalled. Germanicus seems to recognize the error of his concessions (Chapter 40) and decides that his wife and children must leave the camp for safety elsewhere. Their departure is described with great pathos (Chapter 41), so as to account for the change of heart in the troops, a change which Germanicus is quick to capitalize on. Tacitus then gives him a long formal speech (Chapters 42–43), which ensures remorse among the soldiers (it should be remembered that Drusus secured the same result in Pannonia without oratorical skill or the histrionics of attempted suicide). Germanicus then hands over punishment of the allegedly guilty to them (Chapter 44), again in contrast to Drusus who took the matter into his own hands. Tacitus leaves the reader wondering whether Germanicus is fully in command and acting responsibly.

But the mutiny is not over since the two most determined legions are still dissatisfied (Chapter 45) and have to be dealt with. At this critical point Tacitus unexpectedly interrupts the narrative flow to return to Rome and to describe how Tiberius and public opinion were reacting to news of the mutinies (Chapters 46–47). This interruption creates a measure of suspense, since the issue is left unresolved; Germanicus' reported words at the end of Chapter 45 further heighten the uncertainty of the outcome. Tacitus then takes the reader back to Germany for an account of the end of the mutiny among the troops in Upper Germany (Chapters 48–49).

The narrative is once again largely dramatic in presentation. Tacitus doesn't criticize Tiberius' inactivity in his capacity as narrator, but hands criticism over to the *trepida civitas*; this was the sort of thing, he alleges, that people were saying (note *sermones* at 47.1). In response to these alleged criticisms he describes the kind of reflections that Tiberius ought to have been turning over in his mind, 47.1–47.2, another dramatic rather than narrative passage. In Chapter 48 a letter from Germanicus to Caecina is quoted, and Caecina's speech to his loyal troops is reported. Only thereafter is straightforward narrative deployed, to describe the dreadful attack upon the disaffected soldiers. But when Germanicus finally arrives on the scene, speech once again is the narrative medium; with much weeping he deplores the slaughter, a slaughter he himself had recommended in his letter to Caecina, 49.2. The remaining troops are cowed and beg to expiate their civil bloodshed by an attack on the Germans; Germanicus agrees to this and crosses the Rhine, 49.3–49.4.

Tacitus expresses no judgment as historian on the conduct of Drusus and of Germanicus in their management of the Pannonian and the German mutinies, but the very fact that the Pannonian one fizzles out without any concessions having to be granted suggests that Drusus did his job satisfactorily. On the other hand, Germanicus did make concessions to the mutinous troops in Germany (36.3), and his letter to Caecina generated a butchery of Roman troops he could only deplore. Once again, Tacitus passes no express judgment on this, though a weeping general is an unmanly sight. It should also be noted that later he mentions the rescinding of Germanicus' concessions as *male consulta*, 'ill-considered' (78.2).

Style

Roman historians were alive to the need for a prose style suitable for narrating the experiences of the Roman people. However unedifying some events, however reprehensible some of the protagonists, the history of the Roman people was nonetheless, in their view, one of unparalleled distinction and value. No other community had secured and maintained so vast a territorial empire, and that against enemies not only foreign but 'home-grown' as well in a series of civil wars. A second impulse to the creation of prose styles suitable for historiography was rivalry with the Greeks, who had invented and developed history as a literary genre, something distinct from meagre chronicle. Herodotus and Thucydides had in their very different ways produced such distinguished prose that their works were included among the canonic literary monuments of the Greek people. This precedent challenged Roman historians to do something similar for their national literature. And yet until the time of Cicero the challenge was hardly met, at least in Cicero's eyes; historians hadn't yet found styles to match the Greek literary achievement whilst doing justice to the grandeur of the Roman experience. Success was finally achieved not long after Cicero's death by Sallust, who took Thucydides for his model and forged a prose style which in its turn served as a model for Tacitus. Perhaps one aspect of Sallust's style struck Tacitus as especially appropriate for his subject matter. Sallust had focused on moral decline in his two extant monographs on the Catilinarian conspiracy and the war against the Numidian king Jugurtha; even in his now lost masterpiece, the *Histories*, the decline of the Roman state after the dictatorship of Sulla was an important theme. The style he developed for these narratives of national decline was marked by the choice of words either unusual or old-fashioned (archaism; see below), pared down epigrams, and above all a brevity of expression that sometimes produced obscurity. The Sallustian style became fashionable and like all fashions it also found critics. Tacitus will have known the criticisms, but undeterred he seems to have felt that only this style would suit another narrative of decline in the Roman character and morality under the successors of Augustus.

We need to be fair to ourselves and concede that it is nearly impossible to do anything like justice to Tacitean style in English translation, partly because it is one of the most difficult, if not in fact the most difficult, prose styles ever devised by a Roman author. Every resource of the Latin language is brought to bear in order to produce a style both distinctive and distinguished. Tacitus' long apprenticeship as an orator and writer had given him ample practice, and the style of the *Annals* contributes much to the success of his masterpiece. But putting his Latin into comprehensible modern English is no easy matter, and reproducing something of the 'flavour' or tone of his style eludes the resources of contemporary English. In the account which follows focus will first be on some general points, and then on more unusual features of sentence-building and syntax. The problem of satisfactory translation will be kept in view.

History is a literary record of the past, sometimes the remote past, and for that reason Roman historians liked to use antiquated words or word forms, many of which were also to be found in poetry, in a feature called **archaism**. Literary theory, moreover, deemed the writing of history to be close to poetry, so the poetic form of common words or the use of non-standard syntax was acceptable in history to a degree that it would not have been in oratory. A further justification for this practice is that, whilst an oration must be understood as it is being delivered and heard, history is written for a reader, who can be expected to take some time over the nuance of the words.

Perhaps the most commonly used of the old-fashioned word forms is the third-person plural of the perfect indicative active in *–ere*. Everyday Romans had long said (and so wrote) this form in *–erunt*, but historians like poets kept alive the archaic form, as we find in

Chapter 7.2 and 4 *iuravere* and *fuere* and 18.2 *venere* (poets found the form convenient metrically, but historians had no such motive). There is another archaic word-form, *quis* for *quibus* (both dative and ablative plural of the relative pronoun) at 25.2. Tacitus follows other historians in treating unusually the accusative of *vulgus*, normally a neuter noun, as if it were masculine, so we find *vulgum* in 47.3. He also gives an uncommon, poetic sense to the verb *hebesco*, 'grow dim' at 30.3. There is no way English can replicate these features in translation, so we must train ourselves to be alive to their unusual quality as readers of the original Latin text. We see more examples of poetic or archaic colour in a number of words chosen instead of the commonplace ones: 3.5 *ascio* for *ascisco*, 3.6 *tempestas* for *tempus*, 4.1 *aspecto* for *aspicio*, 28.1 *claritudo* for *claritas*, 3.3, 11.4 *cunctus* for *omnis*, and 5.3 *properus* for *celer*. Poetry tended to favour the shorter uncompounded form of verbs, a feature called *simplex pro composito*, and this tendency was picked up by historians; hence at 5.1 *gravescere* for *ingravescere*, at 7.3 *posuit* for *proposuit*, and at 14.3 *solarentur* for *consolarentur*. Once again, these are not features we can hope to reproduce in our translations, but we should aim to acquire a feel for this unusual diction.

Tacitus sometimes avoids everyday or standard expressions. For instance at 3.7 instead of *bella civilia* he writes *bella civium* and at 27.1 *praetorianorum militum* instead of the commonplace *praetorianorum*. We can try to do justice to the former expression at any rate by translating 'citizens' wars' rather than 'civil wars'.

Another characteristic way Tacitus avoids commonplace expression is through the use of **metaphor**, usually in verbal forms. Fire provides him with the commonest source of metaphor: so Agrippa is *ignominia accensum* (4.3), the violence of the mutineers is *flagrantior* (22.1), and the appeal of Vibulenus 'fires up' his audience (*incendebat*, 23.1, cf. *incenderentur* 47.1). Putting on or taking off clothing also serve, the latter at 4.1: *exuta aequalitate*. There is a suggestion at 6.3 *vim* *principatus resolveret* of 'loosening' the reins which control a horse. Finally, and crucially as a device for characterizing the ambiguous Tiberius, metaphors for suppressing and concealing or breaking out are regularly used, as at 4.3 *indicia saevitiae, quamquam premantur, erumpere* and 7.7 *inductam dubitationem*; the metaphor is especially bold at 28.1 *noctem . . . erupturam*. Similarly at 11.2 *verba suspensa*, Tiberius' words are 'up in the air', i.e., hard to pin down, vague.

Latin is a highly traditional language, but the bolder literary spirits exercised some freedom in the **coinage** of new words (again, not something we can reproduce in English). In our extracts there are at least two such coinages, *histrionalis* and *regnatrix*, and they deserve attention. Tacitus doesn't like actors, as becomes more apparent in his account of the reign of Nero, so the new word, which actually first appeared in his *Dialogus*, seems designed to focus the reader's attention on the writer's hostility. Similarly at 4.4 *in domo regnatrice*, 'in the reigning household', *regnatrix* exposes the essential hypocrisy of the principate, which was monarchical in fact if not word.

A peculiar stylistic feature that Tacitus found in Sallust and much developed is **variatio**, the deliberate avoidance of exact balance in contrasted expressions so as to vary the construction. Simple examples are seen at 11.4 *incertum metu* an *per inuidiam* (causal ablative + prepositional phrase), 28.5 *ut novissimi in culpam, ita primi ad paenitentiam*, 47.1 *per Germaniam . . . apud Pannoniam*, 48.2 *in pace . . . ubi bellum ingruat*, and 49.1 where the adverb *palam* is answered by a prepositional phrase *in occulto*. More complex is the variety of expression found at 3.6: *abolendae magis infamiae* (a final gerundive genitive) . . . *quam cupidine* (causal ablative) . . . *aut dignum ob praemium* (prepositional phrase).

Another feature of Sallust's prose style adopted and further refined by Tacitus is the compression of language, sometimes termed **brevitas**, 'concision, terseness'. The simplest form of concision is the omission of a conjunction, called **asyndeton**. Asyndeton is very frequent and serves a range of purposes. It contributes to the punchiness of the narrative, as at 28.4: *se inserunt: spem offerunt, metum intendunt*. That punchiness can be enhanced by **alliteration**, for instance *verba vultus* at 7.7. Lists are commonly presented asyndetically, for instance at 7.1 *consules patres eques*. Finally, asyndeton adds point to antithetical expressions, such at *lacrimas gaudium, questus adulationem* at 7.1. Asyndeton doesn't tend to present us with any problems, but some concise expressions are difficult to translate and occasionally even difficult to understand. At 47.1–47.2, for instance, Tacitus gives vividly dramatic expression to the dilemma confronting Tiberius by listing his reflections as a contrastive series without subordination; the expressions are all attached by apposition to the introductory word *multa*. An impressive example is seen at 49.1–49.2, where the substantive verb 'to be' is omitted throughout, and indeed there are few finite verbs in the passage, which is composed of strings of nouns, varied between abstract and material. Words are simply set down on the page without connection or subordination, so that the reader is left to piece them together into a coherent idea. For instance, the final part of 49.2, *permissa vulgo licentia atque ultio et satietas*, can reasonably be translated as meaning 'the common soldiers were granted a free hand in the exaction of vengeance to their heart's content'. But the equal grammatical weight given to the simple nouns in the nominative case accords to each of them far more force than the English translation has.

Related to this compression is the syntactical figure known as **zeugma**, whereby a word has its proper meaning with only part of the sentence. For instance at 17.4 the verb *redimi* is used in two senses with the objects *saevitiam* and *vacationes*, but with *vestem* we have rather to supply from it the simple verb *emi*. At 49.1 *discedunt* is even trickier, since verbs of quite different sense need to be extrapolated from it to make any sense of *non proelio* and *non adversis e castris* in the earlier part of the sentence. Such compression in Tacitus has been fairly described as 'impressionistic syntax', something we can scarcely manage in our English translations. It is important to appreciate, however, that Tacitus dispensed with words because he felt they were superfluous for the understanding of an alert reader. He isn't trying to flummox us, but rather to keep us on our toes.

The way in which Tacitus builds his sentences has been well compared to a painter's laying on of colours: each phrase is effective in itself and also enhances its neighbours. This is seen most especially in a peculiarity of Tacitean sentence construction, the addition of a 'tailpiece' or coda to an apparently completed sentence. Normally the most important word in a Latin sentence, the verb, is kept to the end or close to the end of the sentence. But Tacitus likes to complete his sentences with the verb(s) and then to add a surprising but highly significant detail in a construction that is, syntactically considered, subordinate. This reversal of the normal and expected pattern compels the reader to focus on the 'tailpiece'. A good example of this is seen in Chapter 3, where Tacitus is listing the individuals who Augustus hoped might succeed him; most of them died prematurely. After all these disappointments Augustus had to go outside his own family and to adopt a step-son, Tiberius, whose preparation for eventual take-over is briskly described by the finite verbs *assumitur* and *ostentatur*, which seem to mark the end of the sentence. Unexpectedly however a clutch of ablatives is added, 3.3 *non obscuris ut antea matris artibus, sed palam hortatu*, which reveal that Augustus wasn't after all sorting the business out entirely on his own, as might have been expected: his wife Livia, who had been mentioned earlier in the sentence, but with hesitation, is now seen to be overtly taking a hand in deciding the succession, which she secures for her biological son, Tiberius. (It may also be noted that this ablatival coda contains a typically imbalanced expression of contrast: *obscuris*)(*palam*.) Tacitus feels the need to illustrate how she had come to wield such decisive influence with Augustus, and so begins the next sentence, 3.4 with the explanatory *nam*. Thus the ablatival tailpiece of 3.3 forms an integral part of the narrative account: it added an unexpectedly important piece of information, Livia's now manifest involvement, and that had to be factored in to the historian's identification of causes. There is a similar 'tailpiece' at 20.1: the sentence seems to end with *insectantur*, but again an ablative phrase, *praecipua ... ira*, is tacked on, so that we focus on the attack upon Rufus, an attack described in detail in a relative clause (*quem ...*); why he was so hated is then explained (20.2). Translators usually treat such tailpieces as independent sentences; this makes sense for modern English, but it forfeits the effects of surprise and of focusing that Tacitus secured.

Particular developments of standard syntax may now be noted; the commentary will explain more commonplace syntactical usage, such as the historic infinitive. It is worth stressing that often there is precedent for Tacitus' practice in the prose usage of Cicero or Caesar or Livy, but we find him pushing the envelope, as it were.

First, then, the usage of cases:

The **accusative** case commonly limits the scope of a verb's action; with verbs of motion it indicates goal. Standard Latin allowed only a few words to stand in the accusative without a preposition to indicate goal (*domus* and *rus*), but poets extended the usage, especially to verbs with a prefix indicating direction. We have examples of this at 13.6 *genua advolveretur* (probably owed to Sallust) and 16.1 *legiones seditio incessit* (again probably owed to Sallust, and taken up before Tacitus by Livy). An alternative explanation of this syntax is that an intransitive verb is used transitively. It should be noted that the 'suppression' of the preposition contributes to that concision of expression which is such a feature of Tacitus' style.

By a kind of analogy to this usage even a verb expressing movement away from a place comes to govern an accusative (or again it may be regarded as transitive): thus at 30.2 *egredi tentoria*, a usage found earlier in Livy.

Finally, other intransitive verbs come to govern direct objects in the accusative. At 4.2 *bellum pavescere* the usage can be explained thus: the function of the accusative is to define or limit the action of the verb, so in this case, where the verb expresses an emotion, the accusative limits the fear to war. At 6.2 *caedem festinavisse* the verb had long been treated by poets as transitive, but here too the limiting function of the accusative is clear: the 'hurried action' is limited to killing.

The **genitive** case tends to define, describe or classify one noun by another; for convenience the particular examples to be described are called the genitive of 'reference', a usage described as 'so much beloved by Tacitus and so often extended in its use'. At 16.1 *licentiam turbarum* the genitive defines the licence as a sort of object, 'licence to riot'. At 17.3 *uligines paludum* the moist ground is defined as swamp; for purposes of translation we can render the genitive adjectivally, 'swampy marsh'. This use of the genitive extends to adjectives as well, especially the so-called 'legal' genitive, an elastic example of which is found at 3.4 *flagitii compertum* 'proved guilty of crime', where Tacitus follows Livy. Other such genitives occur at 7.3 *ambiguus imperandi*, 20.2 *intentus* 'strict' *operis ac laboris*, and 29.1 *rudis dicendi*. At 46.2 *seueritatis . . . summum* the genitive still refers to the particular spheres in which the *princeps* is 'supreme in power'.

The **dative** case normally attaches to verbs and indicates the person 'interested in the action'. A liberal extension of this usage allowed the dative to indicate the agent with passive verbs, a usage favoured by Livy. There is an example at 17.6 *sibi . . . hostem aspici*, where it should be noted that *a se* appears in the first half of the sentence, so Tacitus is avoiding repetition of the same expression of the agent. But the dative case came also to be used with a noun (adnominal) usually to express purpose, a usage developed boldly and frequently by poets and Livy. We have examples at 3.1 *subsidia dominationi*, 22.1 *seditioni duces*, and 24.2 *rector iuveni*, where we should translate with 'for', not 'of', to bring out the force of the case. The notion of purpose is also seen at 29.4 *ostentui* (the bodies are thrown out 'to serve as' a visible warning).

The dative is also attached directly to verbs where classical usage would have a preposition *ad* or *in*, for instance at 23.5 *morti deposcit* 'demanded for death'. Once again we find Tacitus aiming to secure concision of expression.

The **ablative** case performs a number of functions, among which separation or 'place from which' is important. But where classical prose would use a preposition before the ablative, Tacitus uses the simple case, as at 3.3 *remeantem Armenia*, which again produces the concision he liked. The ablative was also used to express a quality, as in 46.2 *principem longa experientia*, 'an experienced *princeps*', as we should say, though Latin usage required an adjective, here *longa*, with the noun denoting the quality. Tacitus departed somewhat from the classical usage, where the quality is not attached directly to a proper name or noun of special reference like *princeps*, but to a generic noun like *vir* in apposition to the name. Yet again we find him reducing the verbiage in favour of a crisper expression. Examples are seen at 13.1 *artibus egregiis* and 24.2 *magna . . . auctoritate*.

We may now turn to some unusual usage of **adverbs**. As the name implies adverbs should normally be attached to verbs but like the dative case they too can be extended to nouns and become 'adnominal'. Examples are found at 3.3 *palam hortatu* 11.3 (where the verbal notion in the noun eases the connection) and 13.1 *fama publice*.

Finally, an observation on Tacitus' use of the **infinitive**. (The developing use of the subjunctive from Livy onwards does not call for comment here, since Tacitus is conforming to the practice of his day.) Once again he is indebted to the practice of poets, who provided him with a precedent for extending the use of the brisk infinitive instead of wordier subordinate clauses. An example is seen at 19.3 *tenderent . . . temptare*, where the infinitive after *tendo* 'aim to' is owed to poetry and to Livy.

Further reading

Birley, A. R. 2000. 'The life and death of Cornelius Tacitus', *Historia* 49: 230–247.

Bowman, A. K., Champlin, E., Lintott, A. (eds) 1996. *The Cambridge Ancient History.* Vol. X, *The Augustan empire, 43 BC–AD 69,* (2nd ed.), Cambridge [contains chapters on 'Expansion of the Empire: the Balkans', 'The Senate and senatorial and equestrian posts' and 'The army and the navy', which help to provide context for the difficulties Tiberius faced in the Senate and with the mutinous armies].

Goodyear, F. R. D. (ed.) 1972. *The* Annals *of Tacitus, Vol. 1 (*Annals *1.1–54),* Cambridge [provides a very detailed account of Tacitus' Latinity and literary presentation].

Hornblower, S., Spawforth, A., Eidinow E. (eds) 2012. *Oxford Classical Dictionary* (4th ed.), Oxford [consult for articles on 'annals, annalists', 'armies, Roman', *decem viri stlitibus iudicandis*; 'historiography, Roman'; quaestor; praetorians; *princeps*; Senate; *tribuni militum*; *tribunicia potestas*; veterans; *vigintiviri*; *vigintisexviri*].

Kraus, C. S. and Woodman, A. J. 1997. *Latin Historians* (Greece & Rome New Surveys in the Classics no. 27), Oxford.

Kraus, C. S. 2009. 'The Tiberian hexad' in Woodman 2009: 100–107 on succession.

Levick, B. 1999. *Tiberius the Politician*, London & New York.

Miller, N. P. (ed.) 1959. *Tacitus*, Annals, *Book 1*, London [gives excellent coverage of the whole of the book].

Oakley, S. 2009. 'Style and language' in Woodman 2009: 195–211.

Seager, R. 2005. *Tiberius*, Malden.

Woodman, A. J., 1998. 'Tacitus on Tiberius' accession' in *Tacitus Reviewed*, Oxford, pp. 40–69 [offers a radically different reading of the opening chapters: Tiberius initially wanted to relinquish the principate entirely and only under pressure proposed power-sharing; Tacitus is careful not to suggest hypocrisy].

Woodman, A. J. (ed.) 2009. *The Cambridge Companion to Tacitus*, Cambridge.

Text

Chapters 1–2: Tacitus offers a rapid summary of the changes in Rome's political structure. He announces his intention to begin his history with a brief account of Augustus' final years, and then to start in earnest from the beginning of Tiberius' principate.

3.　ceterum Augustus subsidia dominationi Claudium Marcellum sororis filium admodum adulescentem pontificatu et curuli aedilitate, M. Agrippam, ignobilem loco, bonum militia et victoriae socium, geminatis consulatibus extulit, mox defuncto Marcello generum sumpsit; Tiberium Neronem et Claudium Drusum privignos imperatoriis nominibus auxit, integra etiam tum domo sua. nam genitos Agrippa Gaium ac Lucium in familiam Caesarum induxerat, necdum posita puerili praetexta principes iuventutis appellari, destinari consules specie recusantis flagrantissime cupiverat. ut Agrippa vita concessit, Lucium Caesarem euntem ad Hispanienses exercitus, Gaium remeantem Armenia et vulnere invalidum mors fato propera vel novercae Liviae dolus abstulit, Drusoque pridem extincto Nero solus e privignis erat, illuc cuncta vergere: filius, collega imperii, consors tribuniciae potestatis adsumitur omnesque per exercitus ostentatur, non obscuris, ut antea, matris artibus, sed palam hortatu. nam senem Augustum devinxerat adeo, uti nepotem unicum, Agrippam Postumum, in insulam Planasiam proiecerit, rudem sane bonarum artium et robore corporis stolide ferocem, nullius tamen flagitii conpertum. at hercule Germanicum Druso ortum octo apud Rhenum legionibus inposuit adscirique per adoptionem a Tiberio iussit, quamquam esset in domo Tiberii filius iuvenis, sed quo pluribus munimentis insisteret. bellum ea tempestate nullum nisi adversus Germanos supererat, abolendae magis infamiae ob amissum cum Quintilio Varo exercitum quam cupidine proferendi imperii aut dignum ob praemium. domi res tranquillae, eadem magistratuum vocabula; iuniores post Actiacam victoriam, etiam senes plerique inter bella civium nati: quotus quisque reliquus qui rem publicam vidisset?

4.   igitur verso civitatis statu nihil usquam prisci et integri moris: omnes exuta aequalitate iussa principis aspectare, nulla in praesens formidine, dum Augustus aetate validus seque et domum et pacem sustentavit. postquam provecta iam senectus aegro et corpore fatigabatur aderatque finis et spes novae, pauci bona libertatis in cassum disserere, plures bellum pavescere, alii cupere. pars multo maxima inminentes dominos variis rumoribus differebant: trucem Agrippam et ignominia accensum non aetate neque rerum experientia tantae moli parem, Tiberium Neronem maturum annis, spectatum bello, sed vetere atque insita Claudiae familiae superbia, multaque indicia saevitiae, quamquam premantur, erumpere. hunc et prima ab infantia eductum in domo regnatrice; congestos iuveni consulatus, triumphos; ne iis quidem annis quibus Rhodi specie secessus exulem egerit aliquid quam iram et simulationem et secretas libidines meditatum. accedere matrem muliebri inpotentia: serviendum feminae duobusque insuper adulescentibus qui rem publicam interim premant quandoque distrahant.

5.   haec atque talia agitantibus gravescere valetudo Augusti, et quidam scelus uxoris suspectabant. quippe rumor incesserat paucos ante menses Augustum, electis consciis et comite uno Fabio Maximo, Planasiam vectum ad visendum Agrippam; multas illic utrimque lacrimas et signa caritatis spemque ex eo fore ut iuvenis penatibus avi redderetur: quod Maximum uxori Marciae aperuisse, illam Liuiae. gnarum id Caesari; neque multo post extincto Maximo, dubium an quaesita morte, auditos in funere eius Marciae gemitus semet incusantis quod causa exitii marito fuisset. utcumque se ea res habuit, vixdum ingressus Illyricum Tiberius properis matris litteris accitur;

neque satis conpertum est spirantem adhuc Augustum apud urbem Nolam an exanimem reppererit. acribus namque custodiis domum et vias saepserat Livia, laetique interdum nuntii vulgabantur, donec provisis quae tempus monebat simul excessisse Augustum et rerum potiri Neronem fama eadem tulit.

6. primum facinus novi principatus fuit Postumi Agrippae caedes, quem ignarum inermumque quamvis firmatus animo centurio aegre confecit. nihil de ea re Tiberius apud senatum disseruit: patris iussa simulabat, quibus praescripsisset tribuno custodiae adposito ne cunctaretur Agrippam morte adficere quandoque ipse supremum diem explevisset. multa sine dubio saevaque Augustus de moribus adulescentis questus, ut exilium eius senatus consulto sanciretur perfecerat: ceterum in nullius umquam suorum necem duravit, neque mortem nepoti pro securitate privigni inlatam credibile erat. propius vero Tiberium ac Liviam, illum metu, hanc novercalibus odiis, suspecti et invisi iuvenis caedem festinavisse. nuntianti centurioni, ut mos militiae, factum esse quod imperasset, neque imperasse sese et rationem facti reddendam apud senatum respondit. quod postquam Sallustius Crispus particeps secretorum (is ad tribunum miserat codicillos) comperit, metuens ne reus subderetur, iuxta periculoso ficta seu vera promeret monuit Liviam ne arcana domus, ne consilia amicorum, ministeria militum vulgarentur, neve Tiberius vim principatus resolveret cuncta ad senatum vocando: eam condicionem esse imperandi ut non aliter ratio constet quam si uni reddatur.

7. at Romae ruere in servitium consules, patres, eques. quanto quis inlustrior, tanto magis falsi ac festinantes, vultuque composito ne laeti excessu principis neu tristiores primordio, lacrimas gaudium, questus adulationem miscebant. Sex. Pompeius et Sex. Appuleius consules primi in verba Tiberii Caesaris iuravere, aputque eos Seius Strabo et C. Turranius, ille praetoriarum cohortium praefectus, hic annonae; mox senatus milesque et populus. nam Tiberius cuncta per consules incipiebat tamquam vetere re publica et ambiguus imperandi: ne edictum quidem, quo patres in curiam vocabat, nisi tribuniciae potestatis praescriptione posuit sub Augusto acceptae. verba edicti fuere pauca et sensu permodesto: de honoribus parentis consulturum, neque abscedere a corpore idque unum ex publicis muneribus usurpare. sed defuncto Augusto signum praetoriis cohortibus ut imperator dederat; excubiae, arma, cetera aulae; miles in forum, miles in curiam comitabatur. litteras ad exercitus tamquam adepto principatu misit, nusquam cunctabundus nisi cum in senatu loqueretur. causa praecipua ex formidine ne Germanicus, in cuius manu tot legiones, immensa sociorum auxilia, mirus apud populum favor, habere imperium quam exspectare mallet. dabat et famae ut vocatus electusque potius a re publica videretur quam per uxorium ambitum et senili adoptione inrepsisse. postea cognitum est ad introspiciendas etiam procerum voluntates inductam dubitationem: nam verba vultus in crimen detorquens recondebat.

Chapters 8–10: During the first meeting of the Senate after Augustus' death, Tiberius discussed the arrangements for Augustus' funeral and the details of his will. Tacitus then offers snippets of public opinion of Augustus' life and achievements.

11. versae inde ad Tiberium preces. et ille varie disserebat de magnitudine imperii sua modestia. solam divi Augusti mentem tantae molis capacem: se in partem curarum ab illo vocatum experiendo didicisse quam arduum, quam subiectum fortunae regendi cuncta onus. proinde in civitate tot inlustribus viris subnixa non ad unum omnia deferrent: plures facilius munia rei publicae sociatis laboribus exsecuturos. plus in oratione tali dignitatis quam fidei erat; Tiberioque etiam in rebus quas non occuleret, seu natura sive adsuetudine, suspensa semper et obscura verba: tunc vero nitenti ut sensus suos penitus abderet, in incertum et ambiguum magis implicabantur. at patres, quibus unus metus si intellegere viderentur, in questus lacrimas vota effundi; ad deos, ad effigiem Augusti, ad genua ipsius manus tendere, cum proferri libellum recitarique iussit. opes publicae continebantur, quantum civium sociorumque in armis, quot classes, regna, provinciae, tributa aut vectigalia, et necessitates ac largitiones. quae cuncta sua manu perscripserat Augustus addideratque consilium coercendi intra terminos imperii, incertum metu an per invidiam.

12.   inter quae senatu ad infimas obtestationes procumbente, dixit forte Tiberius se ut non toti rei publicae parem, ita quaecumque pars sibi mandaretur eius tutelam suscepturum. tum Asinius Gallus 'interrogo' inquit, 'Caesar, quam partem rei publicae mandari tibi velis.' perculsus inprovisa interrogatione paulum reticuit: dein collecto animo respondit nequaquam decorum pudori suo legere aliquid aut evitare ex eo cui in universum excusari mallet. rursum Gallus (etenim vultu offensionem coniectaverat) non idcirco interrogatum ait, ut divideret quae separari nequirent sed ut sua confessione argueretur unum esse rei publicae corpus atque unius animo regendum. addidit laudem de Augusto Tiberiumque ipsum victoriarum suarum quaeque in toga per tot annos egregie fecisset admonuit. nec ideo iram eius lenivit, pridem invisus, tamquam ducta in matrimonium Vipsania M. Agrippae filia, quae quondam Tiberii uxor fuerat, plus quam civilia agitaret Pollionisque Asinii patris ferociam retineret.

13.   post quae L. Arruntius haud multum discrepans a Galli oratione perinde offendit, quamquam Tiberio nulla vetus in Arruntium ira: sed divitem, promptum, artibus egregiis et pari fama publice, suspectabat. quippe Augustus supremis sermonibus cum tractaret quinam adipisci principem locum suffecturi abnuerent aut inpares vellent uel idem possent cuperentque, M. Lepidum dixerat capacem sed aspernantem, Gallum Asinium avidum et minorem, L. Arruntium non indignum et si casus daretur ausurum. de prioribus consentitur, pro Arruntio quidam Cn. Pisonem tradidere; omnesque praeter Lepidum variis

mox criminibus struente Tiberio circumventi sunt. etiam Q. Haterius
et Mamercus Scaurus suspicacem animum perstrinxere, Haterius
cum dixisset 'quo usque patieris, Caesar, non adesse caput rei publicae?'
Scaurus quia dixerat spem esse ex eo non inritas fore senatus preces
quod relationi consulum iure tribuniciae potestatis non intercessisset.
in Haterium statim invectus est; Scaurum, cui inplacabilius irascebatur,
silentio tramisit. fessusque clamore omnium, expostulatione
singulorum flexit paulatim, non ut fateretur suscipi a se imperium,
sed ut negare et rogari desineret. constat Haterium, cum deprecandi
causa Palatium introisset ambulantisque Tiberii genua advolveretur,
prope a militibus interfectum quia Tiberius casu an manibus eius
inpeditus prociderat. neque tamen periculo talis viri mitigatus est,
donec Haterius Augustam oraret eiusque curatissimis precibus
protegeretur.

14. multa patrum et in Augustam adulatio. alii parentem, alii
matrem patriae appellandam, plerique ut nomini Caesaris
adscriberetur 'Iuliae filius' censebant. ille moderandos feminarum
honores dictitans eademque se temperantia usurum in iis quae sibi
tribuerentur, ceterum anxius invidia et muliebre fastigium in
deminutionem sui accipiens ne lictorem quidem ei decerni passus est
aramque adoptionis et alia huiusce modi prohibuit. at Germanico
Caesari proconsulare imperium petivit, missique legati qui deferrent,
simul maestitiam eius ob excessum Augusti solarentur. quo minus
idem pro Druso postularetur, ea causa quod designatus consul Drusus
praesensque erat. candidatos praeturae duodecim nominavit,
numerum ab Augusto traditum; et hortante senatu ut augeret, iure
iurando obstrinxit se non excessurum.

*Chapter 15: Tacitus' account of affairs at Rome in the immediate
aftermath of Augustus' death concludes with details of new procedures
for elections, and arrangements for a festival in honour of Augustus (the
Augustalia).*

16. hic rerum urbanarum status erat, cum Pannonicas legiones seditio incessit, nullis novis causis nisi quod mutatus princeps licentiam turbarum et ex civili bello spem praemiorum ostendebat. castris aestivis tres simul legiones habebantur, praesidente Iunio Blaeso, qui fine Augusti et initiis Tiberii auditis ob iustitium aut gaudium intermiserat solita munia. eo principio lascivire miles, discordare, pessimi cuiusque sermonibus praebere aures, denique luxum et otium cupere, disciplinam et laborem aspernari. erat in castris Percennius quidam, dux olim theatralium operarum, dein gregarius miles, procax lingua et miscere coetus histrionali studio doctus. is imperitos animos et quaenam post Augustum militiae condicio ambigentes inpellere paulatim nocturnis conloquiis aut flexo in vesperam die et dilapsis melioribus deterrimum quemque congregare.

17. postremo promptis iam et aliis seditionis ministris velut contionabundus interrogabat cur paucis centurionibus paucioribus tribunis in modum servorum oboedirent. quando ausuros exposcere remedia, nisi novum et nutantem adhuc principem precibus vel armis adirent? satis per tot annos ignavia peccatum, quod tricena aut quadragena stipendia senes et plerique truncato ex vulneribus corpore tolerent. ne dimissis quidem finem esse militiae, sed apud vexillum tendentes alio vocabulo eosdem labores perferre. ac si quis tot casus vita superaverit, trahi adhuc diversas in terras ubi per nomen agrorum uligines paludum vel inculta montium accipiant. enimvero militiam ipsam gravem, infructuosam: denis in diem assibus animam et corpus aestimari: hinc vestem arma tentoria, hinc saevitiam centurionum et vacationes munerum redimi. at hercule verbera et vulnera, duram hiemem, exercitas aestates, bellum atrox aut sterilem pacem sempiterna. nec aliud levamentum quam si certis sub legibus militia iniretur, ut singulos denarios mererent, sextus decumus stipendii annus finem adferret, ne ultra sub vexillis tenerentur, sed isdem in

castris praemium pecunia solveretur. an praetorias cohortes, quae
binos denarios acceperint, quae post sedecim annos penatibus suis
reddantur, plus periculorum suscipere? non obtrectari a se urbanas
excubias: sibi tamen apud horridas gentes e contuberniis hostem
aspici.

18. adstrepebat vulgus, diversis incitamentis, hi verberum notas, illi
canitiem, plurimi detrita tegmina et nudum corpus exprobrantes.
postremo eo furoris venere ut tres legiones miscere in unam agitaverint.
depulsi aemulatione, quia suae quisque legioni eum honorem quaerebant,
alio vertunt atque una tres aquilas et signa cohortium locant; simul
congerunt caespites, exstruunt tribunal, quo magis conspicua sedes foret.
properantibus Blaesus advenit, increpabatque ac retinebat singulos,
clamitans 'mea potius caede imbuite manus: leviore flagitio legatum
interficietis quam ab imperatore desciscitis. aut incolumis fidem
legionum retinebo aut iugulatus paenitentiam adcelerabo.'

19. aggerebatur nihilo minus caespes iamque pectori usque
adcreverat, cum tandem pervicacia victi inceptum omisere. Blaesus
multa dicendi arte non per seditionem et turbas desideria militum ad
Caesarem ferenda ait, neque veteres ab imperatoribus priscis neque
ipsos a divo Augusto tam nova petivisse; et parum in tempore
incipientis principis curas onerari. si tamen tenderent in pace temptare
quae ne civilium quidem bellorum victores expostulaverint, cur
contra morem obsequii, contra fas disciplinae vim meditentur?
decernerent legatos seque coram mandata darent. adclamavere ut
filius Blaesi tribunus legatione ea fungeretur peteretque militibus
missionem ab sedecim annis: cetera mandaturos ubi prima
provenissent. profecto iuvene modicum otium: sed superbire miles
quod filius legati orator publicae causae satis ostenderet necessitate
expressa quae per modestiam non obtinuissent.

20. interea manipuli ante coeptam seditionem Nauportum missi ob
itinera et pontes et alios usus, postquam turbatum in castris accepere,

vexilla convellunt direptisque proximis vicis ipsoque Nauporto, quod municipii instar erat, retinentes centuriones inrisu et contumeliis, postremo verberibus insectantur, praecipua in Aufidienum Rufum praefectum castrorum ira, quem dereptum uehiculo sarcinis gravant aguntque primo in agmine per ludibrium rogitantes an tam immensa onera, tam longa itinera libenter ferret. quippe Rufus diu manipularis, dein centurio, mox castris praefectus, antiquam duramque militiam revocabat, intentus operis ac laboris et eo inmitior quia toleraverat.

21. horum adventu redintegratur seditio et vagi circumiecta populabantur. Blaesus paucos, maxime praeda onustos, ad terrorem ceterorum adfici verberibus, claudi carcere iubet; nam etiam tum legato a centurionibus et optimo quoque manipularium parebatur. illi obniti trahentibus, prensare circumstantium genua, ciere modo nomina singulorum, modo centuriam quisque cuius manipularis erat, cohortem, legionem, eadem omnibus inminere clamitantes. simul probra in legatum cumulant, caelum ac deos obtestantur, nihil reliqui faciunt quo minus invidiam misericordiam metum et iras permoverent. adcurritur ab universis, et carcere effracto solvunt vincula desertoresque ac rerum capitalium damnatos sibi iam miscent.

22. flagrantior inde vis, plures seditioni duces. et Vibulenus quidam gregarius miles, ante tribunal Blaesi adlevatus circumstantium umeris, apud turbatos et quid pararet intentos 'vos quidem' inquit 'his innocentibus et miserrimis lucem et spiritum reddidistis: sed quis fratri meo vitam, quis fratrem mihi reddit? quem missum ad vos a Germanico exercitu de communibus commodis nocte proxima iugulavit per gladiatores suos, quos in exitium militum habet atque armat. responde, Blaese, ubi cadaver abieceris: ne hostes quidem sepultura invident. cum osculis, cum lacrimis dolorem meum implevero, me quoque trucidari iube, dum interfectos nullum ob scelus sed quia utilitati legionum consulebamus hi sepeliant.'

23. incendebat haec fletu et pectus atque os manibus verberans. mox disiectis quorum per umeros sustinebatur, praeceps et singulorum pedibus advolutus tantum consternationis invidiaeque concivit, ut pars militum gladiatores, qui e servitio Blaesi erant, pars ceteram eiusdem familiam vincirent, alii ad quaerendum corpus effunderentur. ac ni propere neque corpus ullum reperiri, et servos adhibitis cruciatibus abnuere caedem, neque illi fuisse umquam fratrem pernotuisset, haud multum ab exitio legati aberant. tribunos tamen ac praefectum castrorum extrusere, sarcinae fugientium direptae, et centurio Lucilius interficitur cui militaribus facetiis vocabulum 'cedo alteram' indiderant, quia fracta vite in tergo militis alteram clara voce ac rursus aliam poscebat. ceteros latebrae texere, uno retento Clemente Iulio qui perferendis militum mandatis habebatur idoneus ob promptum ingenium. quin ipsae inter se legiones octava et quinta decuma ferrum parabant, dum centurionem cognomento Sirpicum illa morti deposcit, quintadecumani tuentur, ni miles nonanus preces et adversum aspernantes minas interiecisset.

24. haec audita quamquam abstrusum et tristissima quaeque maxime occultantem Tiberium perpulere, ut Drusum filium cum primoribus civitatis duabusque praetoriis cohortibus mitteret, nullis satis certis mandatis, ex re consulturum. et cohortes delecto milite supra solitum firmatae. additur magna pars praetoriani equitis et robora Germanorum, qui tum custodes imperatori aderant; simul praetorii praefectus Aelius Seianus, collega Straboni patri suo datus, magna apud Tiberium auctoritate, rector iuveni et ceteris periculorum praemiorumque ostentator. Druso propinquanti quasi per officium obviae fuere legiones, non laetae, ut adsolet, neque insignibus fulgentes, sed inluvie deformi et vultu, quamquam maestitiam imitarentur, contumaciae propiores.

25. postquam vallum introiit, portas stationibus firmant, globos armatorum certis castrorum locis opperiri iubent: ceteri tribunal ingenti agmine circumveniunt. stabat Drusus silentium manu poscens. illi quoties oculos ad multitudinem rettulerant, vocibus truculentis strepere, rursum viso Caesare trepidare; murmur incertum, atrox clamor et repente quies; diversis animorum motibus pavebant terrebantque. tandem interrupto tumultu litteras patris recitat, in quis perscriptum erat, praecipuam ipsi fortissimarum legionum curam, quibuscum plurima bella tolerauisset; ubi primum a luctu requiesset animus, acturum apud patres de postulatis eorum; misisse interim filium ut sine cunctatione concederet quae statim tribui possent; cetera senatui servanda quem neque gratiae neque severitatis expertem haberi par esset.

26. responsum est a contione mandata Clementi centurioni quae perferret. is orditur de missione a sedecim annis, de praemiis finitae militiae, ut denarius diurnum stipendium foret, ne veterani sub vexillo haberentur. ad ea Drusus cum arbitrium senatus et patris obtenderet, clamore turbatur. cur venisset neque augendis militum stipendiis neque adlevandis laboribus, denique nulla bene faciendi licentia? at hercule verbera et necem cunctis permitti. Tiberium olim nomine Augusti desideria legionum frustrari solitum: easdem artes Drusum rettulisse. numquamne ad se nisi filios familiarum venturos? novum id plane quod imperator sola militis commoda ad senatum reiciat. eundem ergo senatum consulendum quotiens supplicia aut proelia indicantur: an praemia sub dominis, poenas sine arbitro esse?

27. postremo deserunt tribunal, ut quis praetorianorum militum amicorumve Caesaris occurreret, manus intentantes, causam discordiae et initium armorum, maxime infensi Cn. Lentulo, quod is ante alios aetate et gloria belli firmare Drusum credebatur et illa militiae flagitia primus aspernari. nec multo post digredientem cum Caesare ac provisu periculi hiberna castra repetentem circumsistunt, rogitantes quo pergeret, ad imperatorem an ad patres, ut illic quoque commodis legionum adversaretur; simul ingruunt, saxa iaciunt.

iamque lapidis ictu cruentus et exitii certus adcursu multitudinis quae cum Druso advenerat protectus est.

28. noctem minacem et in scelus erupturam fors lenivit: nam luna claro repente caelo visa languescere. id miles rationis ignarus omen praesentium accepit, suis laboribus defectionem sideris adsimulans, prospereque cessura quae pergerent si fulgor et claritudo deae redderetur. igitur aeris sono, tubarum cornuumque concentu strepere; prout splendidior obscuriorve laetari aut maerere; et postquam ortae nubes offecere visui creditumque conditam tenebris, ut sunt mobiles ad superstitionem perculsae semel mentes, sibi aeternum laborem portendi, sua facinora aversari deos lamentantur. utendum inclinatione ea Caesar et quae casus obtulerat in sapientiam vertenda ratus circumiri tentoria iubet; accitur centurio Clemens et si qui alii bonis artibus grati in vulgus. hi vigiliis, stationibus, custodiis portarum se inserunt, spem offerunt, metum intendunt. 'quo usque filium imperatoris obsidebimus? quis certaminum finis? Percennione et Vibuleno sacramentum dicturi sumus? Percennius et Vibulenus stipendia militibus, agros emeritis largientur? denique pro Neronibus et Drusis imperium populi Romani capessent? quin potius, ut novissimi in culpam, ita primi ad paenitentiam sumus? tarda sunt quae in commune expostulantur: privatam gratiam statim mereare, statim recipias.' commotis per haec mentibus et inter se suspectis, tironem a veterano, legionem a legione dissociant. tum redire paulatim amor obsequii: omittunt portas, signa unum in locum principio seditionis congregata suas in sedes referunt.

29. Drusus orto die et vocata contione, quamquam rudis dicendi, nobilitate ingenita incusat priora, probat praesentia; negat se terrore et minis vinci: flexos ad modestiam si videat, si supplices audiat, scripturum patri ut placatus legionum preces exciperet. orantibus rursum idem Blaesus et L. Aponius, eques Romanus e cohorte Drusi, Iustusque Catonius, primi ordinis centurio, ad Tiberium mittuntur.

certatum inde sententiis, cum alii opperiendos legatos atque interim comitate permulcendum militem censerent, alii fortioribus remediis agendum: nihil in vulgo modicum; terrere ni paveant, ubi pertimuerint inpune contemni: dum superstitio urgeat, adiciendos ex duce metus sublatis seditionis auctoribus. promptum ad asperiora ingenium Druso erat: vocatos Vibulenum et Percennium interfici iubet. tradunt plerique intra tabernaculum ducis obrutos, alii corpora extra vallum abiecta ostentui.

30. tum ut quisque praecipuus turbator conquisiti, et pars, extra castra palantes, a centurionibus aut praetoriarum cohortium militibus caesi: quosdam ipsi manipuli documentum fidei tradidere. auxerat militum curas praematura hiems imbribus continuis adeoque saevis, ut non egredi tentoria, congregari inter se, vix tutari signa possent, quae turbine atque unda raptabantur. durabat et formido caelestis irae, nec frustra adversus impios hebescere sidera, ruere tempestates: non aliud malorum levamentum, quam si linquerent castra infausta temerataque et soluti piaculo suis quisque hibernis redderentur. primum octava, dein quinta decuma legio rediere: nonanus opperiendas Tiberii epistulas clamitaverat, mox desolatus aliorum discessione imminentem necessitatem sponte praevenit. et Drusus non exspectato legatorum regressu, quia praesentia satis consederant, in urbem rediit.

Chapters 31–45: Tacitus details the German legions' revolt, and Germanicus' actions. This mutiny was more serious than that among the Pannonian legions; more soldiers rebelled, and more violently, and Tacitus suggests that this mutiny was fuelled by the hope that Germanicus (who at that time had the overall command) would be encouraged by the support of his troops to usurp Tiberius. Germanicus remained loyal to Tiberius, but Tacitus' account encourages criticism of the way he handled the mutiny; by Chapter 45 the immediate crisis point has been dealt with, but the V and XXI legions remain dissatisfied. For further discussion, see Introduction pp.27–30.

AS

46. at Romae nondum cognito qui fuisset exitus in Illyrico, et legionum Germanicarum motu audito, trepida civitas incusare Tiberium quod, dum patres et plebem, invalida et inermia, cunctatione ficta ludificetur, dissideat interim miles neque duorum adulescentium nondum adulta auctoritate comprimi queat. ire ipsum et opponere maiestatem imperatoriam debuisse cessuris ubi principem longa experientia eundemque severitatis et munificentiae summum vidissent. an Augustum fessa aetate totiens in Germanias commeare potuisse: Tiberium vigentem annis sedere in senatu, verba patrum cavillantem? satis prospectum urbanae servituti: militaribus animis adhibenda fomenta ut ferre pacem velint.

47. immotum adversus eos sermones fixumque Tiberio fuit non omittere caput rerum neque se remque publicam in casum dare. multa quippe et diversa angebant: validior per Germaniam exercitus, propior apud Pannoniam; ille Galliarum opibus subnixus, hic Italiae inminens: quos igitur anteferret? ac ne postpositi contumelia incenderentur. at per filios pariter adiri maiestate salva, cui maior e longinquo reverentia. simul adulescentibus excusatum quaedam ad patrem reicere, resistentesque Germanico aut Druso posse a se mitigari vel infringi: quod aliud subsidium si imperatorem sprevissent? ceterum ut iam iamque iturus legit comites, conquisivit impedimenta, adornavit navis: mox hiemem aut negotia varie causatus primo prudentes, dein vulgum, diutissime prouvincias fefellit.

48. at Germanicus, quamquam contracto exercitu et parata in defectores ultione, dandum adhuc spatium ratus, si recenti exemplo sibi ipsi consulerent, praemittit litteras ad Caecinam, venire se valida manu ac, ni supplicium in malos praesumant, usurum promisca caede. eas Caecina aquiliferis signiferisque et quod maxime castrorum sincerum erat occulte recitat, utque cunctos infamiae, se ipsos morti eximant hortatur: nam in pace causas et merita spectari, ubi bellum ingruat innocentes ac noxios iuxta cadere. illi temptatis quos idoneos rebantur, postquam maiorem legionum partem in officio vident, de sententia legati statuunt tempus, quo foedissimum quemque et seditioni promptum ferro invadant. tunc signo inter se dato inrumpunt contubernia, trucidant ignaros, nullo nisi consciis noscente quod caedis initium, quis finis.

49. diuersa omnium, quae umquam accidere, civilium armorum facies. non proelio, non adversis e castris, sed isdem e cubilibus, quos simul vescentes dies, simul quietos nox habuerat, discedunt in partes, ingerunt tela. clamor vulnera sanguis palam, causa in occulto; cetera fors regit. et quidam bonorum caesi, postquam intellecto in quos saeviretur pessimi quoque arma rapuerant. neque legatus aut tribunus moderator adfuit: permissa vulgo licentia atque ultio et satietas. mox ingressus castra Germanicus, non medicinam illud plurimis cum lacrimis sed cladem appellans, cremari corpora iubet. truces etiam tum animos cupido involat eundi in hostem, piaculum furoris; nec aliter posse placari commilitonum manes quam si pectoribus impiis honesta vulnera accepissent. sequitur ardorem militum Caesar iunctoque ponte tramittit duodecim milia e legionibus, sex et viginti socias cohortes, octo equitum alas, quarum ea seditione intemerata modestia fuit.

A Level

Commentary Notes

The notes on the AS set text (Chapters 16–30, pp.47–53) are pitched at an audience just past GCSE, and aim to contain full explanations of syntax and idiom not encountered at GCSE. Key aspects of Tacitean style (such as the use of the impersonal passive) are also introduced and explained here. A broader understanding of Latin is assumed for the notes on the A Level sections. Teachers and students may wish, therefore, to study sections 16–30 first (pp.87–123).

Chapter 3

Tacitus offers in this chapter a sweeping and fast-paced summary of Augustus' attempts to ensure a likely successor. It is worth noting that strict chronology is often ignored.

subsidia dominationi – *subsidia* is in apposition to *Claudium Marcellum ... M. Agrippam ... extulit* – he promoted these men 'as reinforcements for his power'. Despite Augustus' political pre-eminence, it was still important for him to surround himself with loyal men in important positions in order to ensure that this pre-eminence was not questioned. *dominationi* is a superb example of Tacitus' ability to comment through his choice of vocabulary: *dominatio* brings with it connotations of a master/slave relationship; the criticism suggested is that the new powers bestowed upon Augustus as *princeps* were so great that they reduced the other Roman nobles to an increasingly servile role.

Claudium Marcellum – see Index of Persons.

admodum – 'to the limit' and so 'very much a ...'.

A Level

pontificatu et curuli aedilitate – the *pontificatus* was the most important of the priesthoods, and these offices would have been more typically held by senior men. The appointment of Marcellus, therefore, while still an adolescent is indicative of the extent to which constitutional norms were disrupted: power now resulted from the favour of the *princeps*, whereas previously the *cursus honorum* meant that age and seniority were supposed to be linked and that high office should be the result of previous and impressive deeds.

M. Agrippam – see Index of Persons.

ignobilem loco – 'ignoble in birth' – this is further evidence of untypical practice. The Romans were a keenly aristocratic community; a core value for them was the belief that a noble family brought with it an entitlement to power because power should be given to those who had acted nobly in Rome's interests. Men who lacked aristocratic family connections were unlikely to be appointed to top positions.

bonum militia et victoriae socium – note the rhetorical chiasmus (see Introduction, p.10 for the influence of rhetoric on Latin prose authors) and the sharp edge of Tacitus' *variatio*: *bonum* is qualified by an ablative of respect ('good at being a soldier'), whereas *socium* is defined by a genitive noun – 'companion in victory'. The victory referred to is the Battle of Actium, Augustus' decisive victory against M. Antonius.

geminatis consulatibus – 'a double consulship', i.e., Agrippa was consul for two years in succession, something which – because of the Republican principle of shared power – previously had been extremely rare. During the Principate it became an honour typically bestowed only on members of the imperial family.

generum – Agrippa married Julia, Augustus' only child (previously married to Marcellus). As son-in-law, Agrippa gained both the *auctoritas* of belonging to Augustus' illustrious family, and he also stood to inherit Augustus' phenomenal wealth.

privignos – Tiberius and Drusus were Livia's sons by her previous marriage (see Index of members of the Imperial Household).

imperatoriis nominibus: the title 'imperator' brought with it no official *imperium* (i.e., the power that came with office), but did increase the recipients' *auctoritas* (political influence/standing). For the importance of *auctoritas*, see the Introduction p.3.

integra etiam tum domo sua – in effect an ablative absolute with the non-existent present participle of *sum* understood – 'although his own household was still at that time intact'. Augustus' grandsons Lucius and Gaius – now his adopted sons and heirs – were still alive; Tacitus' use of the emphatic *etiam* suggests that in this context Augustus' attempts to line up potential successors were slightly over the top.

genitos Agrippa – the ablative is used to show origin – 'those born from Agrippa', i.e., 'Agrippa's sons'. Augustus adopted Lucius and Gaius in 17 BC.

necdum posita puerili praetexta – the *toga praetexta* (a toga with a purple border) was worn by boys until they officially came of age (at about fifteen) and were ready to wear the *toga virilis*, which was a symbol that they were now old enough to take part in politics and public life. As noted above, Augustus' wish to catapult his grandsons – while still so young – into positions of public prestige is a mark of the change in Rome's values and customs.

principes iuventutis – the title is, of course, an echo of Augustus' own. Gaius and Lucius were elected as *principes iuventutis* by the six squadrons of *equites equo publico*: these squadrons consisted of nobles younger than thirty-five who had not yet held office in the Senate.

Gaius was elected in 5 BC and Lucius in 2 BC; it is noticeable that Tacitus does not mention the time difference. This – together with the emphatic superlative *flagrantissime* – suggests a hot-headed and impetuous wish.

destinari consules – election of consuls some years in advance had become a way of honouring Rome's nobles; Gaius was designated consul in 5 BC (and due to hold office five years later); Lucius in 2 BC.

specie recusantis – 'with the appearance of one refusing' – the people had proposed that Gaius be elected consul in 6 BC, and Augustus refused. Tacitus suggests that his refusal at this time was merely for show.

vita concessit – a grand phrase; the ablative denotes separation.

Armenia – ablative to show motion away from – 'from Armenia'.

fato propera – 'quick by fate', i.e., a death that was early but the result of natural causes.

mors ... vel ... dolus – a key feature of Tacitus' style is the loaded alternative: two options are presented, and our attention is drawn towards one of them. Here, Livia's *dolus* is emphatically left until last. *novercae* assigns to Livia the role of step-mother with all its wicked connotations; N. P. Miller thinks it highly unlikely that Livia had anything to do with Gaius' and Lucius' death. Notice the poetic personification of death.

Nero = Tiberius. Tacitus uses Tiberius as a foreshadower for Nero's cruelty; using Tiberius' *cognomen* here introduces this link at the outset.

illuc cuncta vergere – emphatically pithy and superbly suggestive; the historic infinitive adds further emphasis. For Tacitus' use of the historic infinitive, see note on Chapter 16. The sentence conveys well the new flavour of imperial politics: the deaths of Lucius, Gaius and Drusus cause no overt change in position or office, but now that Tiberius is the sole-surviving heir, and likely therefore to be the next *princeps*, all eyes were on him, and the possibility of complete power shifted in his direction.

filius, collega imperii, consors tribuniciae potestatis – Tiberius was adopted by Augustus in AD 4, and in the same year *tribunicia potestas* was bestowed upon him for ten years; in AD 13 he was given *imperium proconsulare* equal to Augustus (*imperium proconsulare* meant power equal to or greater than any army commander, or any provincial governor). This combination encompassed three key areas of power and influence: as adopted son, Tiberius would inherit Augustus' wealth and the *auctoritas* of his family; *imperium* equal to Augustus' meant jointly superior power within the Senate; the *tribuniciae potestatis* represented the power of popular support. The fourth, and most important, area of power – military command and influence – is emphatically expressed separately and later in the sentence. For further details of Tiberius' military campaigns, see Introduction, p.8.

obscuris . . . matris artibus – ablative of instrument – 'not through the secretive arts of his mother'. Tacitus develops the shadowy and sinister characterisation of Livia.

hortatu – Tacitus has a preference for nouns because they offer a more immediate sense of the action itself, undiluted by reference to time or person. Very effective, therefore, are verbal nouns such as this one, formed from the supine stem of their cognate verb.

devinxerat – again we see Tacitus' preference for metaphor and exaggeration.

unicum – an emphatic adjective.

Agrippam Postumum – Agrippa Postumus (born after Agrippa's death) was Julia's son and Augustus' only surviving direct descendent. After the deaths of Lucius and Gaius, Augustus had adopted him (along with Tiberius) in AD 4 but later disinherited and exiled him.

in insulam Planasiam – Planasia (Pianosa) is a small island lying between Elba and Corsica.

rudem sane bonarum artium et robore corporis stolide ferocem – Agrippa Postumus was notoriously savage and depraved. *bonarum artium* follows *rudem* and refers to the standard skills and characteristics of an educated and distinguished Roman (skills such as rhetoric, military prowess, administrative abilities, legal expertise and characteristics such as commitment to the wider community, respect for others and so forth). *robore* is an ablative of respect used to qualify *ferocem* – 'brutishly confident in his physical strength': the point is that Agrippa Postumus had no good qualities, and relied instead on physical strength as a means of power.

nullius . . . flagitii – genitive used here for the grounds of accusation – 'found guilty, however, of no disgrace'.

at hercule – the surprise is at the contrast: Agrippa (his own grandson) he exiled, but Germanicus – son of Augustus' step-son Drusus – he put in charge of the eight legions in AD 13 (roughly a third of Rome's entire military force at that time), and in AD 4 he made him his adopted grandson.

quamquam esset – in Classical Latin, the indicative is typically used for a concessive clause and the subjunctive suggests thought or opinion, but Tacitus often seems to use it (as here) as the standard mood for this sort of clause.

filius iuvenis – Tiberius' son Drusus, born in 13 BC.

quo – as is usual, *quo* is used to introduce a purpose clause which contains a comparative.

munimentis – notice the military metaphor: the suggestion is that Augustus continues his political career as if a military campaign. The resonance with the Civil War is not complimentary.

ea tempestate – an archaic and poetical equivalent for *eo tempore*.

abolendae … infamiae – dative of purpose – 'to wipe away the shame'.

ob amissum … exercitum – in AD 9 Quintilius Varus suffered an appalling defeat: he committed suicide and the soldiers from his three legions either were killed in battle or massacred afterwards (for the impact of this on the wider army, see Introduction, p.24). Tacitus describes in Chapters 60–62 Germanicus' visit to the site of the defeat and the burial of the remains.

cupidine proferendi imperii – *cupidine* is a causal ablative, and *proferendi imperii* an objective genitive (see Chapter 20 note) – 'because of a desire to extend the empire'.

res tranquillae – understand *erant*.

eadem magistratuum vocabula – an important detail: the names of the political magistracies were the same and – on the surface – Rome was still a Republic. The unstated implication is that only the names were unchanged; the existence of the *princeps* meant that the reality was very different indeed.

inter bella civium – Tacitus likes to avoid standard expressions; here he uses *bella civium* in place of the more usual *bella civilia*.

quotus quisque reliquus – understand *erat*; *quotus quisque* = 'how few'.

qui . . . vidisset – *qui* + subjunctive here as a generic *qui*-clause (i.e., 'of the sort who . . .'). The point is that there is hardly anyone left who had witnessed the Republic properly functioning as such before the Civil Wars; the suggestion is that no one, therefore, was fully aware of what had been lost by Augustus' pre-eminence.

Chapter 4

nihil usquam . . . – understand *erat*.

prisci et integri moris – *integri* is an interesting adjective here: it means 'whole', 'intact' or 'unspoilt'. The suggestion is that the new political set-up is a fractured or polluted version of the previous Republic. The implication is that the pollutant which has caused this damage has been the driving ambition of the nobles at the forefront of the Civil Wars, and indeed of Augustus himself, and the readiness of the other nobles to resign their ambition and be happy with a reduced role of servile obedience rather than leadership.

aspectare – historic infinitive (so too the tricolon of historic infinitives *disserere, pavescere, cupere* below); the verb is poetic, rare and frequentative, and so a striking and emphatic choice of vocabulary.

aetate validus – the ablative *aetate* qualifies the adjective – 'strong in the prime of his life'.

provecta . . . senectus – 'advanced old-age'. Notice the personification of the abstract noun as the subject here.

aegro et corpore – *et* = *etiam* – 'after his now advanced old age was wearied also by bodily illness'.

spes novae – also the subject of *aderat*.

pavescere – *pavesco* is an inceptive verb, i.e., it refers to the beginning of an action – '[more] began to grow frightened'.

differebant – 'distinguished between'; *differo* can also mean 'to spread about', and so 'to spread rumours' or 'to defame'. It is often hard to distinguish between fact and fiction in Tacitus' text and he frequently makes use of reported rumour. This aspect is a key part of his presentation of an age where – in the increasing absence of open debate and free speech – truth became harder to discuss and identify.

trucem Agrippam – understand *esse*. The construction is Oratio Obliqua; Tacitus is reporting the opinions and rumours. *trucem* and *accensum* describe *Agrippam*; *parem* is the complement after the missing *esse*.

non aetate neque ... experientia – the ablatives qualify *parem* – 'equal neither in age nor in experience ...'. It is worth remembering that age had been of little concern to Augustus when he had promoted members of his family to high office (see Chapter 3); these opinions therefore serve as a reminder of general expectations. There is an emphatic contrast, therefore, between expectation and reality.

maturum ... spectatum ... superbia – a pithy tricolon enlivened by the use of *variatio* (adjective, adjective, descriptive ablative). Note that Tacitus gives most attention to the negative characteristic – Tiberius' arrogance – and presents it as an inherited flaw. *superbia* refers to a willingness to step beyond one's entitlements: the position of *princeps* brought with it more power than any one Roman would have been entitled to in the past. Tacitus' criticism, therefore, is an important one: the thirst for power within the new imperial family is presented as integral to the shift from Republic to Principate.

premantur – the present subjunctive is used for vividness in order to retain the tense of the original direct speech (see Chapter 17 note).

A
Level

erumpere – notice the present tense; the signs of savagery were already manifest.

hunc et . . . eductum – understand *esse*. *et* is emphatic – 'this man also . . .'.

in domo regnatrice – the theme of inherited flaws continues. *regnatrice* is found only here, and it is a word resonant with kings and highly critical within a Republican (or indeed pseudo-Republican) context.

congestos . . . consulatus, triumphos – understand *esse*. The statement is hyperbolic: Tiberius held the consulship twice (in 13 and 7 BC), and his military triumphs were fully deserved by his successful military campaigns in Germany and Illyria.

Rhodi specie secessus – *Rhodi* is locative, *specie* is adverbially ablative, and *secessus* is genitive – 'under the facade of a retreat at Rhodes'. For Tiberius' time at Rhodes, see Introduction, p.8.

exulem egerit – 'he played the part of an exile'. *egerit* is perfect subjunctive for the vivid Oratio Obliqua construction (see above, and Chapter 17 note).

meditatum – understand *esse*; this infinitive completes the clause opened by *ne iis quidem annis* – 'not even in those years . . . did he give attention to anything other than . . .'.

iram et simulationem et secretas libidines – these vices are central to Tacitus' later character description of Tiberius, and indeed Tacitus' criticisms of the Principate. In the absence of open and free debate in the Senate, pretence and secrecy thrived.

accedere matrem – 'Then there was his mother'; *accedere* means 'to join the procession' or 'to approach' or 'to be added' – the image is of Livia being close at hand at all times.

A
Level

muliebri inpotentia – descriptive ablative; notice again Tacitus' fondness for abstract nouns. *inpotentia* means both a lack of restraint, and an unmanageability.

serviendum – understand *esse*. The gerundive is used impersonally (for the power of the impersonal construction see Chapter 17 note) – 'There would have to be servitude towards . . .'. The theme of slavery continues.

duobus . . . adulescentibus – i.e., Germanicus (recently adopted by Tiberius), and Drusus, his own son.

qui . . . interim . . . quandoque . . . – *interim* means 'for the time being', i.e., during Tiberius' lifetime, and 'quandoque' means 'at some point', i.e., after his death. The idea is that two sons meant two possible heirs: while Tiberius was alive the state would be squeezed by the need to find suitable honours and benefits for them (see Chapter 3 and the need for a *princeps* to make sure Augustus' likely heirs were so pre-eminent as to be unchallenged at the point of succession); after Tiberius' death there would be the risk of civil war as each of the two vied for the top spot. The present subjunctives *premant* and *distrahant* both refer to the future. The asyndeton creates an emphatic contrast.

Chapter 5

It is now thought to be unlikely that Livia murdered Augustus. Among the ancient historians, Cassius Dio – like Tacitus – suggests that she did; Velleius Paterculus and Suetonius both write that he died of natural causes. Some think that Tacitus' account of Augustus' death is constructed as a foreshadowing of the Emperor Claudius' death, and the beginning of Nero's reign: in both accounts Tiberius/Nero have

A Level

been recently adopted, Augustus/Claudius then show remorse towards a family member, and the wicked mother (Livia/Agrippina) then decides to kill her husband in order to ensure the success of her own son; news of the *princeps'* death is then kept secret until the accession of the adopted son is guaranteed. For a fuller discussion of this, see F. R. D. Goodyear, *The Annals of Tacitus Vol 1*.

agitantibus – understand *eis* (in reference to the general public at Rome). It is in keeping with Tacitus' pithy style that the pronoun is left out.

gravescere – historic infinitive, and another inceptive verb (see Chapter 4 note on *pavescere*).

quippe – 'inasmuch as' – *quippe* denotes cause (cf. its use in a causal *qui* clause).

rumor incesserat – 'a rumour had got underway that . . .'.

Fabio Maximo – consul in 11 BC.

vectum – understand *esse*.

multas . . . lacrimas . . . signa . . . spem – understand *fuisse*; Oratio Obliqua continues as Tacitus reports the rumour.

ex eo – 'from this', i.e., the signs of remorse and affection.

fore ut . . . redderetur – *fore ut* + *subjunctive* is an alternative construction for a future indirect statement (literally – 'it would be the case that . . .') – see *The Oxford Latin Grammar*, p.83.

quod – connecting relative – 'this thing . . .' – it is the object for *aperuisse*.

gnarum id – understand *fuisse*.

neque multo post – *post* = *postea* – 'and not long afterwards'.

dubium an quaesita morte – a phrase typical of Tacitus' compressed style: *dubium an* in Classical Latin typically introduces an indirect question, but in later Latin it is sometimes used adverbially, as here – 'possibly because he had sought his own death' (i.e., suicide was suspected).

semet – an intensified form of *se*.

quod . . . fuisset – 'because she had been . . .'. – as a subordinate clause within Oratio Obliqua the verb is necessarily subjunctive, but there could be a suggestion of an alleged reason too (see *The Oxford Latin Grammar*, p.126).

exitii marito – notice the use of the dative case instead of a genitive; this is possibly to avoid a double genitive, but it also highlights the impact of the death on her husband (cf. the dative of advantage/disadvantage – *The Oxford Latin Grammar*, p.10)

utcumque se ea res habuit – 'whatever the truth of the matter' (literally – 'however that situation had itself').

properis . . . litteris – no doubt the letter was sent at speed, but they must also have urged a fast return.

neque satis conpertum est – 'nor has it been sufficiently clearly established whether . . .'. *utrum* has been left out, but *an* and the perfect subjunctive make it clear that this is a double indirect question.

provisis – the noun for this ablative absolute is missing, and needs to be understood as the antecedent to *quae* – 'when advance action had been taken as the situation required'.

rerum potiri Neronem – '[and that] Tiberius had control of the state'; the use of Tiberius' original cognomen is an acerbic reminder that

Tiberius was not Augustus' own son (after his adoption by Augustus in AD 4 he legally ceased to be a Nero).

fama eadem tulit – 'the same report announced'.

Chapter 6

quibus praescripsisset – the clause reports Tiberius' words, and so follows the rules for Oratio Obliqua – '[he falsely claimed the orders of his father], by which he had given advance instruction to the tribune ...'.

tribuno custodiae adposito – 'the tribune put in charge of the guard'. The *custodia* here refers to the guard placed on Agrippa Postumus.

quandoque – 'at whatever time'. The pluperfect subjunctive *explevisset* represents the future perfect of the original speech which – so Tiberius claims – Augustus gave to the tribune (see *The Oxford Latin Grammar*, pp.86–87).

multa ... saevaque ... questus – *sine dubio* interrupts this pair, and so gives the phrase emphasis. Latin usually has two adjectives and a conjunction; English typically omits the conjunction. The neuter gender is used when the adjective describes the thing that is the action (i.e., 'having complained many savage complainings'), and so in idiomatic English 'having made many savage complaints'.

ut ... sanciretur – the clause provides the object for *perfecerat* – 'he had brought it about that his exile be confirmed by a decree of the Senate'. The resonances of *sanciretur* create a jarring contrast between its core meaning ('to make sacred/inviolable') and its use here in the sense of 'to confirm' in reference to the dubious act of banishing a family member for no known crime (see Chapter 3). The senatorial decree meant that Agrippa's banishment was permanent.

A Level

in ... necem duravit – 'he hardened his heart to the murder ...'. A highly poetical expression: notice the use of metaphor and the abstract noun in a context where prosaic Latin would have used verbs (e.g. 'he decided to kill').

mortem ... inlatam – understand *esse* to create an accusative and infinitive in explanation of *credibile* – 'nor was it plausible that death had been inflicted upon a grandson for the sake of the safety of a step-son'.

propius vero – Tacitus continues the idea introduced by *credibile*; understand *est* – 'it is nearer to the truth that ...', i.e., 'it is more likely that ...'.

Tiberium ac Liviam ... festinavisse – accusative and infinitive again, as above.

novercalibus odiis – the wicked step-mother theme continues (see Chapter 3 note). Tacitus chooses a noun in the ablative case in lieu of a causal clause.

nuntianti centurioni – dative after *respondit*; the present participle is typically used only when the action is strictly contemporaneous with the main verb. The syntax is therefore slightly awkward, and the effect is to suggest a brusque interruption by Tiberius and an uneasy manner.

ut mos militiae – understand *est*. *factum est quod imperasti* was the standard way for soldiers to report that a task had been done. The reference to normal military procedure creates a sharp contrast with this most irregular military mission.

factum esse quod imperasset – *factum esse* forms an indirect statement after *nuntianti*. Its subject is the antecedent for *quod,* and *imperasset* is the shortened form of *imperavisset* ('what he had ordered had been done'). *imperasset* is subjunctive as per the rules for Oratio Obliqua.

A
Level

neque ... et ... – 'both (not) ... and ...'.

imperasse sese – *imperasse* is the abbreviated form of *imperavisse*; *sese* is an emphatic form of *se*.

rationem facti reddendam apud senatum – understand *esse* – '... and that an explanation of the deed must be given before the Senate'.

Sallustius Crispus – great-nephew and adopted son of the historian Sallust; he was an adviser to both Augustus and Tiberius. *particeps secretorum* refers to his role as one of the *amici principis*, the close advisers who were granted admission to the house of the *princeps*; this meant that their discussions had the secrecy of a private conversation (note the contrast with open debate in the Senate).

metuens ne reus subderetur – 'fearing that he might falsely be charged as responsible'.

iuxta periculoso ficta seu vera promeret – another extremely compressed clause. The subjunctive *promeret* shows this to be Oratio Obliqua, and so an indication of Sallustius Crispus' thoughts: *iuxta periculoso* is an ablative absolute ('it being equally dangerous') used in place of the statement needed to complete the conditional, and *ficta seu vera* is equivalent to *sive ficta sive vera*. Altogether it means 'thinking it equally dangerous to produce fiction or truth'.

eam condicionem esse – Oratio Obliqua continues; this statement is the next part of the advice given by Sallustius Crispus to Livia. *eam* is explained by *ut ... constet* – '[he said that] it was a condition of ruling that ...'.

ratio – *ratio* can be a very difficult word to translate; it means a process of reasoning, and so 'reckoning', 'explanation', 'calculation' and so on. Here it is used with *constet* in a financial metaphor – 'the balance-sheet does not add-up unless it is handed over to only one man'. The

A
Level

idea is that if one man wishes to have ultimate power, then he has to accept ultimate responsibility and be willing to make decisions on his own.

Chapter 7

at Romae ... miscebant – Tacitus – like all other Roman nobles – had been trained in rhetoric (see Introduction, p.12). In the *Annals*, however, his prose style usually lacks the smooth and polished balance or neatness of conventional rhetoric. It is a masterstroke that he opens this chapter with two brilliantly rhetorical sentences: the content highlights the servile nature of the Senate, but its style reminds the reader of the age when senators used rhetoric in open debate. Notice the historic infinitive promoted for emphasis, the tricolon in asyndeton, the neat balance of *quanto ... tanto*, the doublets and the neat contrast presented between *laeti ... tristiores, lacrimas gaudium* and *questus adulationem*.

quanto ... tanto ... – 'by the extent to which ... by that extent ...' *quis* is indefinite ('anyone') and so 'the more noble a man was, the more they were disingenuous and in a rush'.

ne laeti ... primordio – the verb needs to be understood – 'so that they did not appear ...'. *excessu* and *primordio* are both ablative to show cause (notice Tacitus' typical preference for nouns in lieu of a causal clause) – 'happy at the death of the *princeps* ...'. *tristiores* – the comparative (as is often the case) is used for emphasis – '... or too sad at the beginning [of another]'.

miscebant – followed by two pairs of direct objects – 'they mixed their tears and their joy, their laments and their flattery'.

A
Level

primi ... iuravere – as is often the case, *primi* in the nominative + a verb means '... were the first to ...'. *iuravere* is the shortened form of *iuraverunt; in verba iuraverunt* means 'swore allegiance to'. The oath did not make Tiberius the *princeps*, but the expression of loyalty from the most senior statesmen did show him to be an undisputed choice.

ille praetoriarum cohortium praefectus, hic annonae – the Praetorian Guard were the only soldiers allowed in Rome; originally they acted as a bodyguard for Rome's generals, but their function gradually changed to a city police force and a personal bodyguard for the *princeps* and his family. Their commander, therefore, was one of the most important men in Rome, and the support of these soldiers crucial to the success of a *princeps*. The *praefectus* of the corn supply was also a crucial figure since corn distributions had become a way to buy mass popular support.

cuncta per consules incipiebat – Tacitus claims that Tiberius made a show of acknowledging the Senate's authority: in the Republic, the consuls took the lead in public discussion. Tacitus suggests that this was disingenuous from the start; it is possible that he is unfair in this interpretation – many have thought that at the start of his reign Tiberius may well have been keen to respect and make use of the Senate as an independent advisory body.

tamquam ... imperandi – *variatio* here marks a return to Tacitus' vigorous and constantly engaging prose style: *vetere re publica* is a descriptive ablative absolute (the non-existent present participle of *sum* needs to be understood) – 'as if the old Republic were still in existence'. It is balanced by a nominative adjective with an objective genitive gerund (see Chapter 20 note) – '... and he was unsure about ruling'.

ne ... quidem ... nisi ... – the negatives cancel each other – 'even the edict ... he issued ...'.

A
Level

tribuniciae potestatis praescriptione – 'under the heading of his tribunician power' – i.e., he summoned the Senate in his role as a *tribunus plebis*. This meant that he acted within the limits of powers previously bestowed on him by the Senate (albeit at Augustus' instigation), and in a way which acknowledged the old Republican conventions.

sensu permodesto – descriptive ablative.

consulturum – understand *se* and *esse* – Oratio Obliqua is used to represent the words of the edict.

neque abscedere a corpore ... – Tiberius was accompanying Augustus' body from Nola to Rome; his only other action was to summon the Senate in order to discuss the honours due to Augustus.

excubiae, arma, cetera aulae – understand *erant*. *aulae* is evocative of Eastern despots and acerbically critical.

miles – the singular noun is used collectively.

adepto principatu – note that the perfect participle of the deponent verb *adipiscor* is here used passively.

causa – understand *erat*.

in cuius manu tot legiones – Germanicus at the time was commander of the eight legions on the Rhine (see Chapter 3). These combined with the auxiliary troops meant that Germanicus had approximately 100,000 men at his disposal and so presented a very real threat; Tacitus seems keen to present him as such, but it is impossible to know whether or not Tiberius viewed him thus at this stage.

dabat et famae ut ... – the literal meaning is 'he was giving it also to public opinion that ...', i.e., 'in deference to public opinion also he wished ...'.

A
Level

vocatus electusque ... videretur – understand *esse* – '[he wished] to appear to have been summoned and chosen ... [rather than] ...'.

uxorium ambitum et senili adoptione – the use of the adjectives *uxorius* and *senilis* is unusual and striking here (more usual would have been to use *uxor* and *senex* in the genitive case).

postea cognitum est – notice that Tacitus offers no source for the claim that follows; it has the status of shady retrospective opinion.

inductam dubitationem – understand *esse*.

nam verba vultus in crimen detorquens recondebat – a dark reference to the *maiestas* trials which blighted the later years of Tiberius' reign.

Chapters 8–10

During the first meeting of the Senate after Augustus' death, Tiberius discussed the arrangements for Augustus' funeral and the details of his will. Tacitus then offers snippets of public opinion of Augustus' life and achievements.

Chapter 11

versae – understand *sunt*.

inde – i.e., after Augustus' funeral. It is generally agreed that the discussion of Tiberius' role and position took place on 17 September AD 14. It is worth remembering that for Tacitus, Tiberius began his role as *princeps* as soon as Augustus died (cf. *primum facinus novi principatus* – Chapter 6); the discussions in the Senate therefore are a further example of the distance between the ongoing façade of the Republic and the reality of one-man rule.

A
Level

preces – Tacitus often exploits the potential of ambiguity, and the content of these prayers is left unreported: the choice of vocabulary encourages the reader to think about them in the context of the prayers at Augustus' death, and the suggestion is that just as the Roman people prayed to the deified Augustus for his continued help and support, they turned now to Tiberius too as the new saviour of their state. There are uncomfortable resonances in this: Tiberius is treated in a way that is quasi-divine, the Roman nobles are presented as devolving themselves of their own responsibility for the governance of their state, and there is a slight hint of self-interest too – Romans making flattering appeals to Tiberius in an attempt to curry favour and shore up their own fortunes.

solam . . . exsecuturos – Oratio Obliqua. Understand *esse* with *solam . . . mentem . . . capacem,* and with *exsecuturos.*

quam arduum . . . regendi cuncta onus – understand *esset* and take *onus* as its subject. *cuncta* is the object of *regendi.* The conventions of historiography meant that historians had a degree of licence in reporting speeches (see Introduction, p.10): notice that here Tacitus encourages a critical reaction from his audience by giving Tiberius the politically loaded verb *rego* instead of the more republican *impero.*

proinde – 'moreover'.

tot inlustribus viris – ablative after *subnixa* (in agreement with *civitate*).

deferrent – subjunctive for a main clause command in Oratio Obliqua (see *The Oxford Latin Grammar,* pp.88–91). *non* is used rather than *ne* because its scope (emphatically) is *ad unum* rather than the verb: 'they should refer everything not to one man'.

sociatis laboribus – ablative of manner – 'with shared enterprise'.

Tiberio – possessive dative; he remains the main focus (hence first word), but making *verba* the subject of the sentence gives them emphasis.

A
Level

quas non occuleret – subjunctive because this is a generic *qui* clause – 'of the sort which he was not keeping secret'.

seu natura sive adsuetudine – causal ablative – 'whether by nature or by habit'.

nitenti – this refers to Tiberius.

ut sensus suos penitus abderet – the suggestion is that Tiberius knew his own sentiments would have been unpalatable to a Rome which was – in appearance at least – still a Republic. With damning ambiguity, Tacitus leaves *sensus* undefined: the primary implication is that Tiberius longs for supreme power within the state, but Tacitus' previous reference to *secretas libidines* (see Chapter 4) encourages the reader's imagination to reach more widely.

in incertum et ambiguum – on the surface Tiberius' words are clear enough. The challenge for the senators is how any genuine system of shared power could be achieved in a state already so geared towards one-man rule: Tiberius had been Augustus' *collega imperii* for the previous ten years and it is hard to see how anyone could now be treated as equal to him.

magis implicabantur – *verba* is still the subject.

quibus unus metus si intellegere viderentur – *quibus* is possessive dative; understand *erat* with *unus metus*. The meaning is that if the senators appeared to understand Tiberius' speech and to acknowledge therefore that power should be shared among them once again, they would be seen to judge Tiberius inadequate for the job. The fear then is that this criticism of Tiberius would result in his animosity .

effundi – historic infinitive; the passive voice emphasises their disempowerment.

ad genua ipsius manus tendere – the distastefully quasi-divine treatment of Tiberius continues; the scene evokes images of Eastern barbarians prostrating themselves in a servile fashion at the knees of their potentate.

cum . . . iussit – an inverted *cum* clause (see Chapter 16 note).

libellum – Augustus is said to have left three written documents when he died: the instructions for his funeral; his account of all he had achieved (the *Res Gestae*), and this summary of the military and financial resources within the Roman empire. See Suetonius *Augustus* 101; Suetonius makes it clear that the documents were produced when the Senate first met to discuss Augustus' funeral. Tacitus makes no mention of this in Chapter 8; it seems that he is conflating the two separate occasions.

quantum – followed by a partitive genitive (see *The Oxford Latin Grammar*, p.8), but in English 'how many citizens and allies were . . .'.

tributa aut vectigalia – *tributum* was the money paid in direct taxation; *vectigalia* were indirect taxes (such as the duties paid on trade, inheritance and so forth).

necessitates ac largitiones – *necessitas* is 'essential expenditure', i.e., the upkeep of roads, armies and so on; *largitio* refers to 'gifts', i.e., things done to ensure good will in the provinces.

quae cuncta – connecting relative – 'all these things . . .'.

incertum – understand *est*.

metu an per invidiam – notice the *variatio* and the emphasis given to *invidiam*; Tacitus implies that Augustus' ambition may have been so great that, not content with total superiority within his own lifetime, he wished no future Roman ever to rule over a larger empire.

Chapter 12

ad infimas obtestationes – 'to the most base entreaties'. *obtestatio* is rarely used; *infimas* is used metaphorically, but its meaning resonates effectively with the image of the Senate prostrate before Tiberius.

senatu ... procumbente – the Eastern image continues.

forte – an interesting detail; the suggestion is perhaps that for the senators there was no way of predicting this, or that Tiberius' ability to negotiate with the Senate was so lacking that an off-hand remark brought consequences which he had not foreseen.

ut ... ita ... – 'just as ..., so ...', i.e., 'even though he was not equal ..., he would even so ...'.

quaecumque ... eius – *eius* refers back to *quaecumque* – '[he would undertake governance] of whatever part ...'.

decorum – understand *esse*.

pudori suo – 'to his own sense of shame', i.e., his modesty.

ex eo cui in universum excusari mallet – *cui* is dative after *excusari*; *in universum* is adverbial – 'from the thing from which he preferred to be excused altogether'.

interrogatum – impersonal passive again – 'the question had been put'.

ut divideret – explains *idcirco* – 'not for that reason ... i.e., so that he might divide', and so 'not for the reason of dividing'.

quae separari nequirent – the object of *divideret* is the antecedent of *quae*, 'things which were not able to be separated'.

sua confessione – i.e., Tiberius'.

A
Level

Tiberiumque ipsum victoriarum suarum quaeque ... admonuit –
admoneo means 'I put someone in mind of something' and so 'he
reminded Tiberius himself of his own victories and the things which
...'. For Tiberius' military victories in Illyria, see Introduction, p.24.

in toga – i.e., matters of peacetime (such as administrative roles) in
contrast to military successes.

fecisset – subjunctive because the clause counts as Oratio Obliqua.

pridem invisus – the structure of Tacitus' narrative here matches
exactly the situation described; Tiberius has already been introduced
as someone whose real thoughts and feelings were impossible to work
out, and who was willing to twist words and expressions into crimes
and store them up for later (see end of Chapter 7); now we find out
retrospectively that Tiberius' feelings (unknown to the reader) were
hostile to Asinius Gallus from the start and for a reason that has no
relevance to the current episode.

Vipsania – for Tiberius' marriage to Vipsania, see Introduction, p.6.

tamquam ... agitaret – *tamquam* + subjunctive gives an alleged
reason (i.e., one which may or may not have been justified) – 'on the
grounds that he aspired to be more than a citizen'.

ferociam – Pollio appears to have been notoriously critical of, and
outspoken about, others.

Chapter 13

quamquam Tiberio nulla ... – understand *erat*; *Tiberio* is possessive
dative.

divitem, promptum, artibus egregiis et pari fama publice – the
object of *suspectabat* – Arruntius – is described by two adjectives and

A
Level

then by two descriptive ablative phrases. *promptus* has a general sense of 'ready for action'; here the implication is 'ready for power'. *artes* refers to the skills and characteristics which would have helped him achieve pre-eminence in the old Republic; *publice* is used as an adverb – 'among the people', and *pari fama* – 'an equal reputation' – means that his reputation was equal to his worth.

quippe – a causal particle, i.e., it shows that Augustus' comments were partly responsible for Tiberius' dislike of Arruntius. In English, 'For Augustus . . .'.

cum tractaret – 'when he was mulling over'.

quinam – *nam* gives emphasis to the interrogative *qui*. The subjunctives *abnuerent, vellent, possent* and *cuperent* all refer to the future, but are imperfect because the clause is generic – 'who would be the sort to . . .'. All are followed by *adipisci principem locum*. The three categories are those who would be up to the task but who would refuse it, those who would not be up to it but who would desire it, and those who both could and would do it.

principem locum – 'the top position', i.e., the role of *princeps*.

suffecturi – the future participle often gives a sense of 'likely to', and so 'who would probably be up to obtaining the top position but would refuse it'.

M. Lepidum . . . capacem – understand *esse*. Marcus Lepidus was consul in A D 6 and had achieved significant military success in Illyria.

si casus daretur – the imperfect subjunctive represents in Oratio Obliqua the present subjunctive of the orginal direct speech conditional clause – 'if the opportunity were given'.

de prioribus – 'about the first two'.

consentitur – impersonally passive (see Chapter 17 note) – 'there is agreement'.

quidam . . . tradidere – *tradidere* is the shortened form of *tradiderunt* – 'some men have reported'.

Cn. Pisonem – Piso was appointed governor of Syria in AD 17 and later accused of poisoning Germanicus there.

omnes – there is a clear over-statement here – *omnes* refers only to two men, one of whom (Gallus) was not arrested until AD 30. Tacitus exaggerates here in order to suggest a vindictive witch-hunt against any whom Tiberius perceived to be a threat.

variis . . . criminibus – 'under various charges'.

struente Tiberio – 'with Tiberius engineering it'. Tacitus makes use of the vivid flavour of the present participle, and the idea of continuous efforts on Tiberius' part to ensure the downfall of these prominent and ambitious Romans.

perstrinxere – the abbreviated version of *perstrinxerunt* and a metaphorical use of the verb.

quo usque patieris – the object of *patieris* is the accusative and infinitive clause (*non adesse caput rei publicae*) – 'How long will you allow there not to be a head for the Republic?'. There is a strong echo of the famously accusatory opening to Cicero's *In Catilinam* I.

ex eo . . . quod – 'from the fact that . . .'. *quod* is followed by a subjunctive (*intercessisset*) because it is a subordinate clause in Oratio Obliqua.

relationi consulum – 'consuls' proposal' – there is no detail about its content, but context suggests that by this stage the consuls had already proposed recognizing Tiberius as Augustus' successor.

iure tribuniciae potestatis – the *tribuni plebis* had the right to veto any motion in the Senate: this right belonged only to the *tribuni plebis* and was one of the most important aspects of their power. Scaurus suggests that because Tiberius did not exercise this right, he gave implicit agreement to the proposal.

flexit – used intransitively – 'he gave ground'.

non ut . . . sed ut . . . – both are result clauses – 'not such that he . . . , but he did . . .'.

fateretur suscipi a se imperium – *suscipi* is a present infinitive because the direct speech would have been *suscipitur a me imperium* (present tense of an agreement, rather than the future tense of a promise). Tacitus is claiming that at no point did Tiberius officially accept his pre-eminent role as *princeps*; Suetonius' account differs (see Suetonius, *Tiberius* 24). The key point here is that although Tiberius would have accepted the individual powers (such as *proconsulare imperium, tribunicia potestas*) which made up his role, Tacitus claims that he did not formally acknowledge that he was therefore at the head of the state; the criticism made is that once again there is distance between appearance and reality.

constat – 'it is agreed'.

deprecandi causa – 'to beg forgiveness'.

advolveretur – the passive of *advolvo* is used when the meaning is intransitive.

interfectum – understand *esse*.

casu – 'by chance'.

donec – followed here by two subjunctive verbs. In Classical Latin, the subjunctive is often used in temporal clauses when the relationship between the temporal clause and the main clause is something a bit more than time alone (see *The Oxford Latin Grammar*, pp.118–121);

A
Level

by the time of Silver Latin it had become the standard mood for many temporal clauses, including those introduced by *donec*.

Chapter 14

multa ... adulatio – understand *erat*. Much is made of Livia's ambition: in Cassius Dio's account there is the suggestion that Livia aimed to share Tiberius' power, but this account may be influenced retrospectively by the ambition of Agrippina, Nero's mother (for more on the parallels between the two *principes*, see Chapter 5 note).

appellandam – understand *esse*.

ut nomini Caesaris adscriberetur 'Iuliae filius' – Tiberius' official title was *Tiberius Caesar Augusti filius*; the suggestion is that this be extended to *Tiberius Caesar Augusti filius Iuliae filius*. This was an extraordinary suggestion in the context of the standard conventions for Roman names.

dictitans – the iterative present participle (see Chapter 20 note).

eadem ... temperantia – ablative after *usurum* (understand *esse*). Tiberius did indeed refuse all unusual honours, such as *Imperator* as a *praenomen*.

anxius invidia – *invidia* is a causal ablative – 'anxious with jealousy'.

et muliebre fastigium in deminutionem sui accipiens – 'and taking a woman's elevation as a diminution of himself'. *sui* is an objective genitive (see Chapter 20 note).

passus est – the object is *ne lictorem quidem ... decerni* – 'not even a lictor to be given [to her]'. The lictors attended high-ranking Romans as a mark of their status. Cassius Dio reports that she had one in her capacity as *sacerdos divi Augusti*.

A Level

aram-adoptionis – the suggestion is that a commemorative altar be built as a monument.

huiusce – *huiusce* is an emphatic form of *huius*.

proconsulare imperium – the *proconsulare imperium* (authority equal to a pro-consul) was the highest level of *imperium* other than the *imperium proconsulare maius of the princeps*. Awarding it to Germanicus would have marked him out as a possible successor.

missi – understand *sunt*.

quo minus . . . postularetur – the clause is one of prevention (see *The Oxford Latin Grammar*, pp.130–132) and it is introduced by *ea causa* with *erat* understood. *quod* here means 'the fact that', and so 'The fact that Drusus was consul designate and present [in Rome] was the reason which prevented the same power being requested for Drusus'. As Consul, Drusus would have *imperium* in Rome; *proconsulare imperium* could not be held in the city at the same time.

hortante senatu ut augeret – increasing the number of praetorships would have allowed more senators to gain the prestige of holding the role.

iure iurando – 'by swearing an oath'.

obstrinxit – used intransitively here – 'he pledged'; *se non excessurum* (understand *esse*) reports his words. In English – 'by swearing an oath he pledged not to exceed [this number]'.

Chapter 15

Tacitus' account of affairs at Rome in the immediate aftermath of Augustus' death concludes with details of new procedures for elections, and arrangements for a festival in honour of Augustus (the *Augustalia*).

A Level

Chapter 16

hic rerum urbanarum status erat – in sections 1–15, Tacitus has written of the very end of Augustus' reign as *princeps* and the beginning of Tiberius'. The constitutional set-up orchestrated by Augustus was a novelty, and so there were no precedents to dictate what should happen after Augustus' death. The handover to Tiberius was extremely significant: it suggested that the position of *princeps* would be hereditary. This gave an even greater monarchical colouring to a constitutional arrangement which was – in theory – still Republican. In the opening chapters, Tacitus acerbically and pointedly highlights the discrepancy between the republican appearance to Rome's politics, and the increasingly monarchical reality, and he vividly reports the confused senatorial debates regarding Tiberius' role and political position. The political uncertainty offered a window of opportunity for the legions to try and better their lot, and Tacitus' choice to order his narrative achieves a strengthening resonance between the disintegration in core Republican values and the disintegration of military discipline.

cum + indicative here for an inverted *cum* clause – grammatically subordinate, but in sense the main clause; this is a construction often used for dramatic and surprising events.

Pannonicas legiones: Pannonia was a province which lay between the Danube and the Austrian Alps (roughly equivalent to modern Hungary).

seditio – a potent word: Rome's recent history had been blighted by violent civil disorder. *seditio* is used here to refer to a military revolt but it is used too of political or civil riots; its resonances bring to mind a centrally destructive part of Rome's political history.

AS

seditio incessit – Tacitus' Latin is highly poetic, and regular use of metaphor is therefore a key part of his style. Here, an abstract noun is made the subject of very concrete and physical verb: the personification of *seditio* therefore creates a metaphorical expression, which strikingly suggests that disorder arose partly through its own momentum.

nullis novis causis – another hallmark of Tacitus's Silver Latin style is his tendency to use nouns rather than verbs; this means that the case system encompasses a wider range of uses than often seen in the Classical Latin of (for example) Caesar or Cicero. Here in lieu of a causal clause, nouns in the ablative case are used: 'nor for any new reasons'. *novis* suggests that conditions for the soldiers have not changed in any significant way – their revolt is not reactive, but rather an opportunistic attempt to better their lot.

nisi quod . . . – 'except for the fact that . . .'.

mutatus princeps – an example of a standard Latin idiom – a noun described by a perfect passive participle, which is best translated in English by an abstract noun: 'the change of *princeps*.' It had taken one hundred years of periodic civil war and unrest to break down the Republic's political principle that power should be shared among Rome's noble elite. The principle of shared rule ran deep, and it was not easy for the competitive and ambitious Roman nobles to accept that they might have no hope of anything better than second place in the political hierarchy. It was entirely conceivable, therefore, that after Augustus' death, there might be others keen for the top spot, and that this might give rise to further civil war.

princeps – another potent piece of political vocabulary – see Introduction, p.2.

licentiam turbarum – a difficult phrase to translate – the vocabulary is deeply pejorative, and once again nouns convey ideas which might otherwise have been expressed by verbs: 'the freedom to riot.'

A S

ex civili bello – in Rome's recent civil wars, rival political leaders bribed soldiers for their support. It is typical of Tacitus' biting style to suggest that the soldiers selfishly might be hoping to profit from something so destructive to their wider community.

ostendebat – Tacitus' style is terse and brief, and he often engages with a wide span of meaning within his words – *ostendebat* here is used in two different senses with its two different objects: '... <u>presented</u> (the opportunity to riot) and <u>brought to mind</u> (the hope of financial reward)'.

habebantur – '... were quartered'. The three legions referred to were VIII Augusta, XV Apollinaris and IX Hispana.

ob iustitium aut gaudium – *iustitium* refers to a suspension of public business: this was a standard way to mourn the death of a major statesman; *gaudium* at the start of a new *princeps'* reign could also be an appropriate reaction, but the pair of opposite emotions creates an uneasy sense of mixed feelings and uncertainty.

eo principio – 'from that beginning'.

lascivire ... discordare ... praebere ... cupere ... aspernari – historic infinitives, i.e., an infinitive used as the main verb. The power behind this construction is that the infinitive – as a verbal noun – focuses on the thing that is the action itself, undiluted by reference to person or time. Tacitus' tendency to use historical infinitives is in keeping with his liking for the punchiness of nouns.

miles – used in the singular to refer to the soldiers as a group (cf. the old English 'soldiery').

pessimi cuiusque – *quisque* + superlative = 'all the ...' and so here 'all the worst men'.

denique luxum et otium cupere, disciplinam et laborem aspernari – the neat balancing contrast within this creates an epigrammatic conclusion (see influence of rhetoric on Tacitus' style – introduction p.10).

dux . . . theatralium operarum – Percennius had been the leader of a theatre claque, i.e., a group of men hired to whip up applause for one actor and to jeer at his rivals. Support for different actors was akin to support for a modern day football team: emotions at the theatre could run high.

procax lingua et miscere coetus histrionali studio doctus – note the Tacitean *variatio* (see Introduction, p.34) – the first adjective *procax* is qualified by a descriptive ablative ('shameless in speech'), and the second adjective *doctus* by an explanatory infinitive ('practised in stirring up'). *histrionali* is a word found only in Tacitus. The theatre was seen as a rather low-grade event; there is nothing complimentary about Tacitus' character description here.

is imperitos . . . congregare – a murky and congested sentence: Tacitus' syntax often mirrors his sense, and here ellipsis and varied syntax reflect the secretive and multiple meetings. The two historic infinitives *inpellere . . . et . . . congregare* provide the main verbs; *quaenam . . . condicio* is an indirect question with its verb omitted (– *nam* as a suffix provides emphasis: 'what indeed the condition of service would be . . .'). *conloquiis* is an instrumental ablative ('by means of meetings'), and two different constructions give a timeframe for these: the adjective *nocturnis,* and the ablative absolute *flexo . . . die. deterrimum quemque* – 'all the worst men'.

Chapter 17

promptis iam et aliis seditionis ministris – *et* is emphatic – 'also'.

contionabundus – a very rare word, and – like *seditio* – one which resonates with the political sphere. Percennius is like someone addressing a political assembly.

interrogabat – this introduces a passage of extended indirect speech (Oratio Obliqua – see *The Oxford Latin Grammar,* pp.82–85), which lasts until the end of this chapter. All main clause statements use the accusative and infinitive construction; the subjunctive is used for all subordinate clauses.

ausuros – understand *esse*. The infinitive shows that this is a rhetorical question, since in Oratio Obliqua rhetorical questions follow the rules for indirect statements, not indirect questions.

nisi . . . adirent – 'if they did not make an approach to'. The imperfect subjunctive represents the future simple of the original direct speech.

precibus vel armis – there is plenty of rhetoric here (note how this doublet balances *novum et nutantem*), but it is also an example of Tacitus' ability to colour our response. The more damaging option – the use of force – comes second.

peccatum: understand *esse*. The infinitive is impersonally passive, a verb form where the subject is the action itself. It is very close therefore to a noun and often best translated as such 'there had been [enough] mistakes', or 'enough had gone wrong'. (Compare with e.g. the very common *fortiter pugnatum est* – 'fighting was fiercely fought' and so 'there was a fierce battle'.)

quod . . . tolerent: note the subjunctive's vivid present tense; rather than following the strict rules of sequence (see *The Oxford Latin Grammar,* pp.86–87), Tacitus has retained the tense of the original direct speech.

senes et plerique truncato . . . corpore – Tacitean *variatio* again – the soldiers are described by an adjective and a descriptive ablative absolute.

AS

dimissis – in 13 BC the fixed term for military service was sixteen years within a legion, and four years thereafter in a veteran brigade (see below). In AD 6 this fixed term increased to twenty years' service within the legion. Upon discharge, the soldiers would receive a fixed sum of money – in theory 12,000 sesterces. In practice, however, there was often not enough money available in the treasury to pay this discharge fee and so soldiers were often kept on as veterans for much longer periods. The rebellions described in *Annals* I brought about a return to the principle that soldiers should be discharged after sixteen years plus four as a veteran, but a year later Tiberius requested that military service be extended again to twenty years.

apud vexillum tendentes – soldiers who had completed their term of service within the legion were often kept as veterans under a separate military standard (*vexillum*). In theory they were exempt from various regular duties and they were only to be called upon in case of attack; Percennius suggests otherwise. *tendentes* implies *tentoria tendentes* – 'stretching their tents' and so 'quartered'.

si ... superaverit: – the perfect subjunctive belongs to primary sequence; as for *tolerent*, Tacitus has vividly retained the tense of the original direct speech rather than following the rules of sequence.

vita – ablative and adverbial: 'if anyone survived with his life', i.e., 'if anyone lived through'.

trahi – the present infinitive used for general truth – 'If anyone lived through . . . , they would be dragged . . .'.

diversas in terras – 'to remote lands'. Land to farm was often allocated as part of the discharge package when there was not enough money available to pay it in cash, but – unsurprisingly – it was typically in rather uninhabited areas and not very desirable in quality.

AS

enimvero militiam ipsam gravem – supply *esse. enimvero* gives a strong affirmative tone to the statement; expressive words such as this and *an* (see below) were a common feature of rhetoric.

denis . . . assibus – the ablative case is used for price.

in diem – 'a day'.

hinc – 'from this [sum of money]'. Soldiers had to pay their way from their allocated pay: Tacitus' list moves from the stuff of daily necessity (clothes, military equipment, board and lodging) to the need to pay to ease the harsh conditions of military service.

redimi – used in different senses – clothing etc/respite from duties <u>were bought</u>, but the centurions' savagery was <u>paid off</u>.

saevitiam centurionum – centurions were allowed to beat the soldiers; no doubt many abused this privilege.

at hercule – this exclamation marks the contrast between the need to buy daily the things which might ease a soldier's life, and the everlasting nature of the difficulties of military service *(sempiterna)*.

verbera . . . sempiterna – understand *esse*.

exercitas aestates – campaigns were typically waged in the summer; during winter months, legions were quartered and engaged in tough training exercises.

sterilem pacem – 'sterile' in the sense that no benefit came from peace.

nec aliud levamentum – understand *esse*.

ut . . . mererent – a result clause – 'such that they earned a denarius per day'. There were sixteen *asses* in one *denarius*, so this marks a significant increase from the daily pay of ten *asses* mentioned above.

A S

sextus . . . adferret – a command within Oratio Obliqua, 'the sixteenth year should bring . . .'. Tacitus now lists the other demands Percennius encouraged the soldiers to make, and the imperfect subjunctive is used throughout to mark this construction.

praemium – discharge package – 'their discharge should be paid in cash'.

an – this adds an indignant tone to the rhetorical question – 'or is it that . . .'.

praetorias cohortes – the Praetorian Guard were the soldiers based in Rome. As the principate established itself, they rapidly became equivalent to the emperor's personal bodyguard. It is not surprising that to soldiers stationed elsewhere in the empire they appeared to have rather a comfortable deal.

binos denarios – 'two denarii a day'.

penatibus suis – 'their own homes and families'.

sibi – the dative is placed prominently at the start of the clause to emphasise the contrast between the Praetorian Guard and the legionary soldiers – 'but for them'.

aspici – present passive infinitive.

Chapter 18

diversis incitamentis – ablative of cause: 'for various reasons'.

exprobantes – 'displaying in accusation'.

eo furoris – 'to such a pitch of frenzy'.

venere – the shortened form of the 3rd pl. perfect *venerunt*. This abbreviation is common in verse, and a hallmark of the archaic style favoured by Sallust, Tacitus' forerunner. For the resonances between Tacitus' prose style and Sallust's, see Introduction, p.31.

tres legiones miscere in unam – this is a remarkable proposal. The identity of each legion – symbolised by the eagle and the legion's military standards – inspired fierce loyalty from its members.

eum honorem – 'that distinction', i.e., the honour of being the legion which gave its name and identity to the new super-sized legion.

aquilas – the silver or gold eagle was the symbol of the legions, and each legion carried one together with its military standards.

quo magis . . . foret – as is usual, *quo* introduces a purpose clause which contains a comparative. *foret* = *esset*.

properantibus – 'while they were hurrying to finish this'.

clamitans – 'repeatedly shouting'.

legatum – *legatus* means a deputy or ambassador, but it became the standard title for a commander of a legion, in so far as the commander of each legion was the appointed deputy to the overall commander of the army.

quam – the Latin here is compressed; in English translate as 'than if . . .'.

imperatore – the choice of title here is a reminder that the *princeps* – as supreme commander – should be obeyed by all Romans.

Chapter 19

pectori usque – to chest-height.

cum . . . omisere – *omisere* is the abbreviated form of *omiserunt* (see Chapter 18 note); *cum* is used here again with the indicative for an inverted *cum*-clause (see Chapter 16 note).

multa dicendi arte – 'with great rhetorical skill' (NB genitive of gerund, as is usual when the gerund is used in conjunction with another noun – see *The Oxford Latin Grammar*, pp.108–112). Note the contrast created between Percennius and Blaesus: in keeping with his higher social rank, Blaesus speaks with the refined polish expected of an educated Roman.

non . . . desideria . . . ferenda ait – *ait* is typically used with direct speech, but not so here: understand *esse*.

neque . . . petivisse: the construction shifts to Oratio Obliqua (see Chapter 17 note).

veteres – 'their predecessors'.

ab imperatoribus – 'from their commanders'.

a divo Augusto – Julius Caesar had been deified in 42 BC. The Senate awarded Augustus the honour of the same title.

tam nova – the soldiers were demanding conditions of service better than had been known for a very long time.

parum in tempore – 'not at a good time'.

incipientis principis curas – a typically brief phrase: Latin often uses verbs where English would use nouns: 'the concerns of a *princeps* at the start of his reign'.

quae – 'things which' – the antecedent is omitted.

civilium . . . bellorum victores – the soldiers on the winning side of the previous civil wars were in a strong position: their commander owed his power to them. The soldiers of the VIII, IX and XV legions in no way had such a hold over Tiberius.

expostulaverint – the speech moves into primary sequence, and so vividly retains the tenses of the original direct speech (see note on Chapter 17).

contra morem obsequii, contra fas disciplinae – a smoothly polished and balanced phrase. *fas* refers to divine law, i.e., actions which are incontrovertibly the right thing to do; combined with *disciplinae* the sense is that military discipline requires absolutely that soldiers be obedient to their commanders. In English: 'contrary to the custom of obedience, contrary to the unbreakable rules of military discipline.'

decernerent – the subjunctive in a main clause in Oratio Obliqua represents a command – 'they should choose.'

legatos – 'representatives.'

se . . . coram – 'in his presence.'

adclamavere – the abbreviated form for *adclamaverunt* – '[The soldiers] shouted their approval.'

tribunus – each legion had six military tribunes (*tribuni militum*) who carried out the day-to-day administrative duties of the legion. Unlike positions such as centurion, which were filled from the rank and file soldiers, the military tribunes were appointed from Rome's upper classes (cf. the traditional distinction between officers and soldiers in the British Army).

ab sedecim annis – 'after sixteen years.'

mandaturos – understand *esse*. The accusative and infinitive construction is used since this sentence is part of the soldiers' reply to Blaesus. 'They said that they would send other demands . . .'.

provenissent – subjunctive as is usual for subordinate clauses within indirect speech. The pluperfect tense represents here the future perfect indicative in the original direct speech.

modicum otium – understand *erat*. *otium* usually means leisure, or freedom from activity; here it means that the soldiers stopped their agitations: 'there was short-lived calm'.

superbire miles – *miles* – collective singular (see Chapter 16 note). The infinitive is an emphatic historic infinitive: 'the soldiers became arrogant'.

quod . . . obtinuissent – a complicated sentence – once again syntax mirrors sense and the grandiosely complicated structure mirrors the haughty thoughts of the soldiers. *quod* is followed by a subjunctive because the clause represents the soldiers' thoughts and so follows the rules for subordinate clauses in Oratio Obliqua. *orator publicae causae* is in apposition to *filius*: 'the son of the *legatus* – as advocate for the common cause – was proof enough . . .'. *expressa* is an infinitive (with *esse* understood); its subject (*ea* – understood) is then described by the relative clause *quae . . . obtinuissent*, which has a subjunctive verb in keeping with the rules for subordinate clauses in Oratio Obliqua. '. . . that by force things had been extorted which they would not have achieved through restraint.'

Chapter 20

manipuli – a maniple was a small division within the Roman army; three maniples made up one cohort.

ante coeptam seditionem – again the perfect passive participle is best translated with a noun in English (see Chapter 16 note): 'before the beginning of the military revolt.'

A S

Nauportum – a town in modern Slovenia (Vrhnika).

ob itinera et pontes et alios usus – another prepositional phrase used in lieu of a clause – 'for the reason of roads and bridges and other necessities' means 'in order to work on roads, bridges etc'. Road-making was an important military task: good roads meant a better supply chain and faster communication, but building the roads was also a useful way of keeping the soldiers occupied.

postquam turbatum ... accepere – *accepere* for *acceperunt* – 'they received news'. *turbatum* (with *esse* understood) is an indirect statement; the infinitive is impersonally passive and best translated with a noun 'that there was uproar' (see Chapter 17 note).

vexilla convellunt – 'they uprooted their standards'. While soldiers were occupied in one location, their standards were fixed in the ground; uprooting them was a symbol that the troops were now on the move again and no longer engaged with the work they should have been doing.

direptis – 'ransacked'. Note the difference between *dis/di* as a prefix and *de*: *dis-* represents separation and dispersal, whereas *de-* signifies removal (cf. *dereptum* later in this chapter).

retinentes – 'trying to stop them'.

insectantur – 'they ran at'.

praecipua in Aufidienum Rufum ... ira – another ablative phrase relating to *insectantur* – 'their anger directed especially towards Aufidienus Rufus'.

praefectum castrorum – this was a senior position; technically in charge of the camp's administration, the *praefectus castrorum* could be sent out with smaller groups of soldiers to lead them in the field. Aufidienus Rufus is in charge of these maniples.

primo in agmine – 'at the head of their marching column'

per ludibrium – 'as a jeer'.

rogitantes – 'repeatedly asking'. This is an example of a verb used in its iterative form; note the *–ito –itare* ending (cf. *clamitantes* in Chapter 18).

an – 'whether'. In a direct question *an* supplies an indignant tone, and this is carried through into this indirect version.

ferret – two different senses here: 'to carry' and 'to endure'.

quippe – 'the reason was that'.

castris – dative here after *praefectus*, since the root verb (*praeficio* – to put in charge of) is followed by a dative.

intentus – followed here by a genitive (see Introduction, p.38) – 'strict about'.

eo inmitior quia: a construction similar to *eo inmitior quo* … ('less lenient to the extent to which …') but with a stronger sense of cause – 'all the more cruel because …'.

Chapter 21

circumiecta – perfect passive participle in place of a noun – 'the surrounding areas'.

ad terrorem ceterorum – another example of Tacitus' tendency to express actions through nouns rather than verbs – the sense is 'to frighten the others'.

adfici . . . claudi – both are present passive infinitives after *iubet*.

carcere – Tacitus often uses nouns without prepositions to express place; here the ablative case denotes 'in prison'.

legato ... parebatur – impersonal passive (see Chapter 17 note) – 'there was obedience towards the commander'.

optimo quoque – superlative + *quisque* (see Chapter 16 note) – 'all the best men'.

illi – as is typical when this pronoun is used at the start of a sentence, *illi* marks the change in subject to those who were arrested.

obniti ... prensare ... ciere – historic infinitives. The sentence structure here is dramatic and full of action (note the use of present participles), in keeping with the soldiers' frantic appeals.

ciere ... nomina singulorum – 'they called individuals by name'. *centuriam, cohortem,* and *legionem* then follow as further objects of *ciere;* the extended list of objects echoes the frantic series of appeals tumbling out in fast succession.

centuriam quisque cuius manipularis erat – 'each man called upon the century of which he was a member'. A *centuria* was made up of one hundred men, and formed 1/60 of the legion.

eadem omnibus inminere – indirect statement after *clamitantes* (notice the iterative form of the verb – see Chapter 20 note).

nihil reliqui faciunt quo minus ... permoverent – a difficult construction – *reliqui* is partitive genitive after *nihil* – 'they did nothing of the remainder by which the less ...' and so 'they left nothing undone in order to ...'.

adcurritur – impersonal passive again and historic present for a vivid focus on this action – 'there was an onrush'.

rerum capitalium damnatos – the genitive supplies the cause of the conviction – 'condemned (to death) for capital offences', i.e., crimes that carried with them the death penalty.

AS

Chapter 22

flagrantior inde vis – understand *erat*. Notice the use of metaphor: *vis* – personified – is described by an adjective typically used of fire, and often used pejoratively of moral vices such as unbridled lust.

apud turbatos et quid pararet intentos – *intentos* here is qualified by an indirect question – 'among men in disorder and keenly interested in what he was about to do'.

lucem et spiritum – now released from the military jail, the prisoners are back in the light and fresh air, but *lux* and *spiritus* are both often used to refer to life itself (the light of life, the breath of life). There is a neat contrast between their restoration to freedom and the impossibility of bringing Vibulenus' supposedly dead brother back to life.

a Germanico exercitu – i.e., from the army stationed in Germany.

iugulavit – Blaesus is the subject.

in exitium militum – *in* denotes purpose here (notice again Tacitus' use of a prepositional phrase in place of a clause) – 'for the destruction of his soldiers'.

abieceris – perfect subjunctive for an indirect question in primary sequence (see *The Oxford Latin Grammar*, pp.94–95).

cum . . . implevero – 'when I have sated . . .'. *cum* is followed here by the future perfect indicative; the indicative is the standard form when *cum* refers to present or future time; the future perfect tense here denotes an action which will take place in the future, but which will be completed prior to the action in the main clause.

dum . . . sepeliant – *dum* + subjunctive often carries a sense of purpose or intention (cf. 'wait <u>until</u> I get back'), and here this is best expressed by 'provided that ...' or 'so long as ...'. *hi* refers to the bystanders, and *interfectos* to Vibulenus and his brother.

Chapter 23

incendebat – Vibulenus is the subject; notice that the fire metaphor continues.

fletu et ... verberans – *variatio* again: *incendebat* is qualified by the ablative noun *fletu* and by the present participle *verberans*. *fletu* is a good example of Tacitus' propensity to use nouns, even when referring to actions.

disiectis – as is typical of Tacitus' compressed style, the noun described by this participle has been left out; understand *eis* for this and also as the antecedent for *quorum* – 'when the men had scattered on whose shoulders ...'.

praeceps – a very compressed phrase – the adjective 'headlong' is used to convey the sense 'falling headlong'.

pedibus – ablative to show place (or possibly dative after *advolutus*) – 'at the feet'.

advolutus – the passive provides an intransitive sense – 'rolling around'.

tantum – 'so much' – using the neuter adjective here as a noun followed by a partitive genitive places greater emphasis on the quantity.

e servitio – 'among Blaesus' slaves'.

ceteram ... familiam – *familia* here refers to 'household', and so to Blaesus' other slaves.

AS

effunderentur – the passive voice is used again for the intransitive meaning of the verb – 'they poured forth'. Note again Tacitus' use of metaphor.

ac ni propere . . . pernotuisset – *ni* for *nisi* – 'and if it had not quickly become clear that'; three separate accusative and infinitives then need to be translated – *corpus . . . reperiri, servos . . . adnuere, fuisse . . . fratrem.*

adhibitis cruciatibus – it was expected that slaves would be loyal to their masters, and so evidence from slaves was typically acquired using torture.

illi – possessive dative – 'there had never been to him a brother', i.e., 'he had never had a brother'.

haud multum ab exitio legati aberant – Classical Latin would use a subjunctive for the main clause here after the subjunctive conditional clause (see *The Oxford Latin Grammar*, pp.114–117), but Tacitus opts for the indicative. The effect is a stronger and more vivid statement of fact in place of the suppressed subjunctive main clause. *haud multum . . . aberant* – 'they were not far away from' and so 'they came very close to', and *would have done so*, had it not become clear that . . .

extrusere – archaic form of *extruserunt* (see Chapter 18 note).

sarcinae . . . direptae – understand *sunt*; note the ellipsis helps the fast pace of the narrative.

interficitur – a striking shift mid-sentence to the vivid historic present.

cedo alteram – *cedo* here is an old imperative form (*do* compounded with the emphatic particle *ce*) and so 'Give me another!'.

vite – the vine-rod was the mark of the centurion's office, and it was the means by which he exercised his right to flog his men.

AS

ceteros latebrae texere – a very poetic clause – *texere* is the archaic form of *texerunt*, and the personification of *latebrae* as the subject of the verb is typical of poetry. *tego* means 'to hide' or 'to conceal' and it often – as here – has a sense of 'to protect'.

uno – 'alone'.

qui ... habebatur idoneus – *habebatur* here means 'was thought / considered'; *idoneus* is followed here by a dative noun and gerundive – *perferendis ... mandatis* – 'for relaying the requests ...'.

promptum ingenium – 'quick intellect', i.e., he was good at thinking on his feet.

quin – 'indeed' – the word is emphatic.

inter se – 'against each other'.

ferrum parabant – 'were making ready their swords'; *ferrum* is used in the singular and supplies a focus therefore on the iron blade of each sword. This use of the singular is common in poetry.

dum ... illa deposcit – *illa* refers to the VIII legion. *deposcit* is followed by an accusative and then a dative (of purpose) – in English the idiom is different – 'while the VIII legion was demanding their centurion's death'. The *dum* clause carries a slight sense of cause.

tuentur – historic present (cf. *deposcit*).

ni ... interiecisset – once again, the syntax here is very compressed. *nonanus miles* refers collectively to the soldiers of the IX legion. *adversum aspernantes* refers to the soldiers of the VIII and XV legions and uses a preposition + participle in place of a longer clause ('to counter them when they scorned ...'). *ni* (for *nisi*) *interiecisset* is a conditional clause (see *The Oxford Latin Grammar*, pp.114–117), but its main clause needs to be understood: 'if the soldiers of the IX legion had not intervened with entreaties and – when the soldiers scorned these – threats, then …'. The idea is that the VIII and XV legions would indeed have fought each other, were it not for the intervention of the IX legion.

Chapter 24

quamquam … occultantem – a very Tacitean piece of syntax. Unlike authors such as Cicero and Livy, Tacitus is loath to weigh his prose down with extended subordinate clauses. *quamquam* would typically introduce a concessive clause (i.e., a clause that shows the events in the main clause to be slightly surprising), but here it is used to give a concessive flavour to the description embedded in the main clause.

abstrusum et tristissima quaeque maxime occultantem – *variatio* (note the use of an adjectival perfect passive participle and then a present participle), the two superlatives (*tristissima* and *maxime*) and the unusual use of *abstrusum* (this is the only known use of it to describe a person) attract our attention to this significant character description. Tiberius returns here to Tacitus' stage; the description Tacitus gives him, coloured by deceit and disguise, is not flattering. One of the central criticisms Tacitus makes of the principate is that it lacked the honesty of the previous Republic: despite the façade of senatorial debate, decisions were increasingly not made through open and public discussion, but they were subject instead to the private whim of the *princeps*.

tristissima quaeque – superlative + *quisque* again – 'all that was most grievous'. The power of Tacitus' analysis often rests just as much on ambiguity as direct comment; here, the reference of *tristissima* is left open: did Tiberius conceal things that were grievous to him, or to others, or both?

perpulere – archaic form of *perpulerunt* (see Chapter 18 note).

ut . . . mitteret – result clause.

praetoriis cohortibus – see Chapter 17 note.

nullis satis . . . consulturum – the syntax is hurried and staccato in structure, and Tacitus' preference for phrases instead of clauses is clear; once again, syntax mirrors sense and reinforces the suggestion that Tiberius acted quickly but without sufficiently careful forethought. *nullis satis certis mandatis* – understand *datis* or similar; *nullis satis certis* reveals Tacitus' opinion – the event described is that Tiberius sent Drusus free to respond as the situation required; the comment Tacitus makes suggests a lack of clear direction and a weakness in Tiberius' leadership. *consulturum* – the future participle is used where we might otherwise expect an indirect command or an expression of purpose – 'he was to take thought' (cf. the use of the future participle to express purpose in Greek). *ex re* – 'as the situation required'.

cohortes – i.e., those from the Praetorian Guard which were sent with Drusus.

delecto milite – *miles* is used once again as a collective noun, see Chapter 16 note.

supra solitum – the perfect participle is used here, but – once again – is translated best in English as noun – 'beyond their usual size' (see Chapter 16 note).

robora Germanorum – a metaphorical phrase; *robur* means hard wood, such as oak, and so 'the strength of the German troops', and therefore 'the best of . . .'. The soldiers (mainly from Batavia) formed a private bodyguard to the imperial family.

Aelius Seianus – a key player in the later events of Tiberius' reign – see Introduction, p.18. He is mentioned here for the first time. *additur* needs to be understood.

collega Straboni – the Praetorian Guard was commanded by two *praefecti* of equestrian rank.

magna apud Tiberium auctoritate – descriptive ablative. *apud* usually means 'in the presence of'; here the best translation is 'he had great influence over Tiberius'. *auctoritas* is a crucial piece of political vocabulary (see Introduction, p.3): Latin distinguishes between different sorts of power: *potestas* is the capability to do something; *imperium* is the temporary power that comes with a particular office or role; *auctoritas* is the power of influence possessed by an individual. In the new principate, the Roman state was subject not just to the whims of the *princeps*, but also to the opinions of those whom the *princeps* listened to most closely. For Tacitus, the importance of *auctoritas* in the new regime is another key area to criticize.

rector . . . ostentator – as in Chapter 16, Tacitus uses the conventions of rhetoric (note the chiasmus here) to give a neat epigrammatic end to his description. *ceteris periculorum praemiorumque ostentator* has a powerful whisper of ambiguity: Sejanus' role was to make clear to others the risks and benefits brought by disobedience and obedience respectively. There is another message here too: his own position reveals very clearly the rewards of personal loyalty to the *princeps*, and the dangers that might bring to others.

Druso propinquanti – dative after *obviae fuere*.

fuere = *fuerunt*.

laetae . . . fulgentes . . . inluvie deformi et vultu – the *variatio* here (adjective, participle, descriptive ablative) is emphatic.

insignibus fulgentes – soldiers were awarded *insignia* (cf. modern-day medals) for individual displays of bravery and prowess. They were worn on formal occasions.

quamquam ... imitarentur – the natural mood for a concessive clause is the indicative; when the subjunctive is used (as here) the flavour suggested is something possible / hypothetical rather than real: their appearance was sorrowful, but this was just a façade.

contumaciae propiores – this descriptive detail provides a powerful coda at the end of the sentence (see Introduction, p.36 for other examples).

Chapter 25

vallum – the *vallum* surrounded the camp; earth was piled into a high rampart, and a defensive fence set on top.

firmant – the soldiers are the subject; the atmosphere is threatening, and the scene is made more vivid by the use of the historic present and three main verbs in asyndeton.

globos – *globus* refers to a mass or a group; it is not a standard term for a division of the Roman army. The choice of vocabulary therefore highlights that the soldiers' actions here are out of the ordinary.

certis castrorum locis – the ablative case used without a preposition to denote place.

illi – notice how the focus has jumped from Drusus to the soldiers, back to Drusus and again to the soldiers. One of conventions of Latin prose writing is to maintain a smoothness of style by keeping the same subject throughout a passage where possible. Tacitus' writing here is therefore unusually jumpy: once again, syntax mirrors sense and, just as the soldiers look at each other, then Drusus, then back at each other, so too does the reader.

quoties ... rettulerant – the pluperfect is the standard tense for a frequentative time clause in the past (i.e., 'whenever they moved their gaze back ...'). It would usually be followed by an imperfect tense in the main clause, but Tacitus chooses instead to use a historic infinitive for vividness and drama (see Chapter 16 note).

Caesare: Drusus – Tacitus uses *Caesar* as name for both the *princeps* and his sons.

murmur incertum, atrox clamor et repente quies – understand *erat* with each phrase. There is Tacitean *variatio* here: the noun and adjective pattern is broken with the use of an adverb in the last pair.

litteras – *littera* in the singular refers to a letter of the alphabet; *litterae* in the plural refers to a written letter.

in quis – archaic equivalent to *in quibus* (see Introduction, p.32).

praecipuam ... curam – indirect statement – understand *esse*. Oratio Obliqua (see note on Chapter 17 and *The Oxford Latin Grammar*, pp.82–85) is used to relay the contents of the letter; the construction lasts until the end of the chapter. *ipsi* is possessive dative, and *fortissimarum legionum* an objective genitive (genitive used to supply an object for a verbal idea contained in another noun or adjective) – 'there was particular concern to him for ...' and so 'he had particular concern for ...'.

quibuscum ... toleravisset – *toleravisset* is subjunctive because it is a subordinate clause within *Oratio Obliqua*. Tiberius had been commander of the armies in Pannonia from 12–9 BC, and again during the Illyrian Revolt of AD 6–9.

ubi primum – 'as soon as'.

requiesset – a shortened form of the pluperfect subjunctive *requievisset*.

acturum apud patres – understand *esse* – 'he would bring the matter before the Senate'. It is usual for subject of the infinitive to be expressed, but context makes it quite clear that Tiberius is the subject here, and the accusative masculine ending *actur<u>um</u>* confirms this. *patres* was a standard term for the senators, dating from the Romulus foundation myth. In this myth, Romulus established the Senate with one hundred men, named *patres* to represent their role as fathers of Rome's various clans.

quae – the antecedent is omitted – 'those things which'.

tribui – present passive infinitive (after *possent*).

cetera ... servanda – understand *esse* – 'the other demands were to be kept for the Senate'.

quem ... haberi par esset – 'whom it was fair to consider practised both in indulgence and in strictness'.

gratiae ... severitatis – difficult words to translate. *gratia* usually refers to the benefit which arises from a kind act, but here refers to the Senate's disposition to act kindly or indulgently. *severitas* therefore refers to the opposite of this, i.e., the Senate's ability to be strict in refusing requests made.

Chapter 26

responsum est: impersonal passive (see Chapter 17 note) – 'The response was ...'.

mandata – understand *esse* for the indirect statement which follows *responsum est* – 'that instructions had been given'.

quae perferret – the subjunctive denotes purpose – 'which he was to relay'.

de missione . . . haberentur – for the soldiers' demands, see notes on Chapters 16–19.

ut . . . foret – *foret* = *esset* and with *ut* forms an indirect command – '[he said] that there should be . . .'.

ad ea Drusus cum . . . obtenderet – translate as *cum Drusus ad ea . . . obtenderet*.

clamore turbatur – an unusual use of *turbo* in the passive: Drusus is the subject – 'he was assailed with shouts'. Notice the singular abstract noun *clamor* used here to represent the many shouts of the mob.

cur venisset – the subjunctive shows that Tacitus has moved to Oratio Obliqua (see Chapter 17 note) and we now hear the angry shouts of crowd.

neque augendis militum stipendiis neque adlevandis laboribus – dative of purpose – 'neither for increasing the soldiers' pay, nor for reducing their labours'.

nulla bene faciendi licentia – again, Tacitus' propensity for nouns is evident, and he uses the ablative case here to denote attendant circumstance. Very literally the Latin means 'with no licence for acting well'; in better English the sense is 'he did not have the power to do any good'. *faciendi* is genitive, as is usual when the gerund is used in connection with another noun (*licentia*).

verbera et necem . . . permitti – accusative and infinitive for a main clause within Oratio Obliqua.

cunctis – there is a hyperbole here – in fact, only the provincial governor could order a soldier's death.

Tiberium . . . frustrari solitum – understand *esse*.

nomine Augusti – 'in the name of Augustus' – i.e., Tiberius – as an excuse not to act – had claimed that decisions had to be referred to Augustus.

easdem artes – object of *rettulisse*. It is comparatively unusual for the accusative object to precede the accusative subject of the infinitive, but it deserves its place here at the start of the sentence because *easdem artes* is the link between this sentence and the previous one.

filios familiarum – the technical term for the minors of a family, and so a contemptuous choice of vocabulary: the implication is that Drusus is too young to be of any use.

venturos – understand *esse* and its subject (indicated by *venturos*) – 'would anyone ever come'.

novum id plane quod – 'it was certainly a novelty that ...'. *novum* is sarcastic. *quod* + indicative is often used to mean 'the fact that ...'; the subjunctive here is because the clause is within Oratio Obliqua. The present tense subjunctive marks a vivid shift to the tense of the original direct speech (rather than following the strict rules of sequence – see *The Oxford Latin Grammar*, pp.86–87 and Chapter 17 note).

eundem ... senatum consulendum – understand *esse*. Latin often uses a word in agreement with the subject when English would more naturally use an adverb – 'the same Senate should be consulted' and so 'the Senate should be consulted in the same way'.

sub dominis – 'within the power of their rulers'. *dominus* was a potent and pejorative choice of vocabulary: Tacitus' main criticism of the principate is that the Romans became in effect slaves to the will of one man. Augustus and Tiberius made great efforts to present the Senate as an independent and important part of government; Tacitus often suggests that this was disingenuous.

sine arbitro – 'without an arbitrator' – i.e., subject to whim and without controls.

Chapter 27

ut + subjunctive for a frequentative time clause: 'whenever any of the Praetorian guard or Drusus' entourage came their way'.

causam discordiae et initium armorum – the accusative nouns here are used in apposition to *manus intentantes*, i.e., the act of making threatening gestures was 'the starting point for strife and the beginning of violence'. *armorum* refers of course to weapons, but the sense requires the reader to think beyond the weapons to the fighting they were used for.

maxime infensi Cn. Lentulo – *Lentulo* is dative after *infensi* – 'hostile to'. This is probably a reference to Cn. Cornelius Lentulus, who was consul in 14 BC and had campaigned against the Dacians.

ante alios aetate et gloria belli – 'ahead of others in age and military glory'.

illa militiae flagitia – 'those actions so shameful to the army'.

primus – 'first' and so 'in first place', and therefore 'particularly'. It is common for Latin to use adjectives in agreement with the subject of the verb, where English would more naturally use an adverb (see Chapter 26 note).

digredientem eum Caesare – *Caesare* is used in the ablative and without a preposition to denote motion away from 'as he was heading away from Drusus'.

provisu periculi –*provisu* is used in the ablative in lieu of a causal clause – 'with foresight of the danger'.

rogitantes – frequentative form (see Chapter 20 note) – 'asking again and again'.

ad imperatorem an ad patres: understand *utrum . . . an . . .* – 'whether to their commander (i.e., Tiberius) or to the Senators'.

AS

exitii certus – 'sure he would die'. Notice again the use of an abstract noun (*exitium*) where English naturally would use a verb.

Chapter 28

noctem – Tacitus opens his sentence with the accusative object, and thus emphasizes that night/darkness is his main focus here: the adjective and participle (*minacem* and *erupturam*) powerfully personify the night. The personification of something like the night is a literary trope found more often in poetry (notice also the personification of *fors*), as is the metaphor contained in *in scelus erupturam*. Tacitus develops this poetic flavour in the next clause: *luna claro repente caelo visa* – here the words which refer to the moon appear intermittently in the sentence. Word order mirrors sense ('enactment'), and this is a poetic technique used by Virgil in particular. There is a potent irony in this scene: lunar eclipses usually were thought to portend disaster for those in authority, but here it helps them.

languescere – historic infinitive (see Chapter 16 note). This lunar eclipse took place at about 5am on 27 September AD 14.

rationis ignarus – *rationis* is an objective genitive (see Chapter 20 note) – 'unaware of the reason'. *ratio* refers to the rational explanation for the eclipse; amongst the uneducated and superstitious soldiers it seemed to be a sign from the gods.

suis laboribus – a compressed phrase. The comparison is between the failure of the moon, and the failure of their own efforts.

prospereque ... redderetur – the construction is Oratio Obliqua because it relates the soldiers' opinion (see Chapter 17 note); Latin can mark this shift through syntax alone, while in English a verb such as 'believing' needs to be supplied. *esse* should be understood with *cessura*, and the accusative subject of this infinitive is the omitted antecedent for *quae* ('the things which … would turn out …'). *redderetur* is the historic sequence equivalent for what would have been a present subjunctive in the direct speech conditional clause (see *The Oxford Latin Grammar*, pp.86–87 and pp.114–117): 'if brilliance and brightness were restored for the goddess …'.

strepere – historic infinitive, as are *laetari* and *maerere*. The idea was to use noise to distract away from the moon the magic power responsible for the eclipse.

splendidior obscuriorve – these comparatives describe the moon; Tacitus omits the verb, so it needs to be understood: 'as the moon grew brighter or darker'.

offecere – the abbreviated form of the perfect indicative *offecerunt*.

creditum – understand *est* – 'it was believed'.

conditam – understand *lunam* and *esse* for the indirect statement which follows *creditum*.

ut – *ut* + indicative – 'in the way that …'.

sua facinora aversari deos – the accusative object of the infinitive is emphatically placed before its accusative subject: 'the gods were turning away from their crimes in disgust.'

utendum … iubet – the word order is unusually dislocated here – take *Caesar ratus* first. The focus shifts to Drusus, but we hear the first part of his plan before he is mentioned: the effect is to imply rapid thinking on Drusus' part. *utendum inclinatione ea* is an indirect statement after *ratus; esse* should be understood; the gerundive of obligation is impersonal (necessarily so because *utor* takes the ablative – see *The Oxford Latin Grammar*, p.112) – 'there must be a using of that inclination', and so 'he must make use of that inclination'. *vertenda* also needs *esse* to be understood; it is in agreement with the omitted antecedent for *quae* – i.e., 'those things chance had offered should be turned into . . .'. *sapientiam* – Tacitus uses the abstract noun here to emphasize the idea of good sense; the meaning however is that the soldiers should be encouraged to return to obedience and loyalty, and that this was a much more sensible course of action.

et si qui alii – 'and any others who were . . .'. Understand *erant*.

grati – 'pleasing to' and so 'influential'. *bonis artibus* marks a contrast with Percennius and Vibulenus.

inserunt . . . offerunt . . . intendunt – one might expect an indirect command here to relay the instructions given by Drusus to these men. Tacitus leaps instead to the fulfilment of these orders (vividly described with the historic present tense). This jump aids the sense of speed in this passage.

quis certaminum finis – understand *erit*.

pro Neronibus et Drusis – Nero and Drusus were the two surnames for the *gens Claudia*; the plural is used to denote their applicability to all members of the family.

quin potius . . . sumus – *quin* emphasizes the contrast: 'why don't we rather be [the first to show repentance]'.

in culpam . . . ad paenitentiam – notice again Tacitus' propensity to use emphatic abstract nouns. Classical Latin would be more likely to use verbs, since the idea is one of action – the soldiers have acted wrongly; they should now regret it. Tacitus uses prepositions to careful effect: *in* shows movement into (i.e., they have actually done something wrong); *ad* suggests movement towards (i.e., they should show regret, but they are not there yet).

AS

tarda sunt – the compressed style continues; the adjective requires us to understand an accompanying verb – 'slow <u>to be granted</u>'. The noun described is the omitted antecedent to *quae* – 'those things which . . .'.

mereare – the abbreviated form of the present subjunctive 2nd sg *merearis*. The subjunctive is used gently to suggest a possible action – 'you might earn private thanks immediately'. *privatam* refers to something done on an individual basis in contrast to something done as part of a group.

statim recipias – the suggestive tone is heightened – 'immediately you might get them', i.e., receive the benefit of loyal action, but no direct mention is made as to how that loyalty might be rewarded.

inter se suspectis – 'suspicious of each other'.

tironem – a young soldier or a new recruit.

redire – historic infinitive.

signa – for the military standards and their significance, see Chapter 18 note.

principio seditionis – 'at the beginning of the revolt' – *principio* is ablative to denote time when. Notice that Tacitus opens and closes this episode with the politically resonant word *seditio* (see Chapter 16 note).

Chapter 29

rudis dicendi – *rudis* is used here with a genitive gerund (a use similar to the objective genitive, or the genitive which typically follows adjectives such as *imperitus*) – 'unpractised in speaking'.

nobilitate ingenita – ablative of quality. The relationship between rhetoric, class and power is an interesting one: status in Rome had

A S

long depended upon power and influence (either personal, or that possessed by ancestors) and – in the Republic – power and influence had depended partly on the ability to persuade. Rhetorical skill was, therefore, the cornerstone of an aristocratic Roman's education. Interestingly, Tacitus suggests here that although Drusus is too young to be a fully polished and accomplished speaker, his noble birth brings with it a natural authority which is enough to carry his point.

negat se . . . vinci – notice the present tense infinitive – 'he said that he was not being won over by . . .'.

si videat, si . . . audiat – for vividness, the tense of the original direct speech is retained; these represent the present subjunctives of the original speech – 'If I were to see . . .' (see *The Oxford Latin Grammar*, pp.114–117).

scripturum – understand *se* and *esse*.

placatus – the perfect passive participle subordinates what is really the first of Drusus' intentions: he offers to write to his father to placate him and so that his father then will hear the soldiers' requests in a more favourable state of mind.

orantibus – understand *eis*.

rursum idem Blaesus – *idem* because this is the same man sent before (see Chapter 19).

primi ordinis centurio – the *primi ordines* were probably the six centurions from the First Cohort, and the leading centurion from each of the other nine cohorts.

certatum inde sententiis – understand *est* with *certatum*; for the impersonal passive construction (see Chapter 17 note) – 'Then there was a battle of opinions'. The *sententiae* belong to those advising Drusus in the camp.

opperiendos legatos – understand *esse* as an indirect statement (containing a gerundive of obligation) after *censerent*.

permulcendum militem – understand *esse* again.

agendum – understand *esse*. *agendum* is used impersonally – 'the situation should be handled'.

nihil ... auctoribus – Oratio Obliqua. Tacitus is rarely impartial in his writing: here – as is often the case – he offers competing viewpoints, but weights his narrative on one side by offering more detail for one than the other. Here, the opinion of those calling for tougher solutions is relayed in extended Oratio Obliqua: this is the opinion, therefore, that the reader remembers.

nihil ... modicum – understand *esse*. As previously noted, the syntax makes the Oratio Obliqua clear in Latin; in English we need to understand 'they said ...'.

ni paveant – present tense subjunctive. Tacitus is again using the vivid construction, where the tense of the direct speech is retained. This subjunctive therefore represents the present indicative of the original direct speech.

ubi pertimuerint – as above, the perfect subjunctive represents the perfect tense of the original direct speech – 'ubi pertimuerunt, inpune contemnuntur'. The perfect indicative is rare for a verb such as *timeo* which, denoting a state of being, leans towards the imperfect tense. Here the perfect tense shows that *ubi* means 'whenever' (see *The Oxford Latin Grammar*, p.120) and it should be translated in English as a present tense: 'whenever they are frightened, they can be ignored with impunity'.

adiciendos ... metus – *metus* is accusative plural; understand *esse*. In English, the noun works more naturally in the singular; the implication here is that lots of soldiers will feel fear, hence the plural noun.

tradunt plerique – Tacitus offers two endings to this episode; notice that the more critical of the two is given emphasis at the end of the sentence. Note *tradunt* here means 'report'.

obrutos – understand *esse*. Vibulenus and Percennius are the subjects.

abiecta – understand *esse*.

ostentui – a striking final word. Tacitus uses a noun in the dative case to express purpose ('for show') rather than a purpose clause; the effect is pithy and direct.

Chapter 30

quisque praecipuus turbator – 'each leading agitator'; the Latin focusses on each rabble-rouser as an individual, but the natural English idiom is to use the plural – 'all the leading agitators'.

conquisiti – understand *sunt*. The verb is plural because of the plural group denoted by *quisque praecipuus turbator*.

documentum fidei – *documentum* in apposition to the action (see Chapter 27 note) – they handed over the soldiers 'as proof of their loyalty'.

tradidere – shortened form of *tradiderunt*.

tutari signa – since the military standards were the symbol of the legion, it would be a very bad omen if they were damaged in the storm.

unda – *unda* refers to any water in motion, so here 'flood-waters'.

et formido – *et* here is emphatic – 'in addition'.

AS

nec frustra . . . redderentur – Oratio Obliqua – Tacitus relays their fearful thoughts. In English, add 'they believed that'.

sidera – the plural is used for a general statement, but the immediate reference is to the lunar eclipse (see Chapter 28).

non aliud . . . levamentum – understand *esse*. Translate *aliud* with *quam si . . . linquerent* – 'there was no remedy for their troubles other than to leave . . .'.

soluti piaculo – *piaculum* refers to any expiatory offering, and so by extension to the sin itself.

quisque . . . redderentur: *quisque* is nominative singular, referring to each man individually; *redderentur* is plural because it refers to all the soliders as a group.

hibernis – their winter camps.

rediere – abbreviated form of *redierunt.*

nonanus – understand *miles* (as a collective noun).

opperiendas . . . epistulas – understand *esse* for an indirect statement after *clamitaverat. epistulas* is plural in form, but singular in meaning (cf. *litterae*).

clamitaverat – the iterative form of *clamo* (pluperfect tense) – 'repeatedly had been shouting'.

aliorum discessione – Tacitus uses a noun where Classical Latin would use a temporal clause.

imminentem necessitatem – without the support of the other legions, the IX legion had little hope of successful disobedience; return to usual duties was therefore the only option.

et – emphatic – 'and Drusus too'.

AS

Chapters 31–45

Tacitus details the German legions' revolt, and Germanicus' actions. This mutiny was more serious than among the Pannonian legions; more soldiers rebelled, and more violently, and Tacitus suggests that this mutiny was fuelled by the hope that Germanicus (who at that time had the overall command) would be encouraged by the support of his troops to usurp Tiberius. Germanicus remained loyal to Tiberius, but Tacitus' account encourages criticism of the way he handled the mutiny; by Chapter 45 the immediate crisis point has been dealt with, but the V and XXI legions remain dissatisfied. For further discussion, see Introduction.

Chapter 46

Tacitus' account of Tiberius' thoughts and motivations must be at best invention; note however that the historiographical tradition allowed historians a fairly free hand in reconstructing speeches, and it is an interesting extension of this for Tacitus here to detail Tiberius' thoughts.

cognito – the 'noun' described by this participle is the entirety of the indirect question (*qui . . . Illyrico*); in English it is best translated as '[Since at Rome] they had [not yet] discovered'.

qui – interrogative (note the subjunctive *fuisset*) and in agreement with *exitus*.

Illyrico – *Illyricum* is used here, slightly inaccurately, to describe the region within which Pannonia was.

civitas – i.e., the citizens as a group.

incusare – historic infinitive.

AS

quod . . . dissideat . . . queat – the verbs are subjunctive because this is virtual Oratio Obliqua, i.e., the reason for the state's criticism of Tiberius is being reported. For vividness, Tacitus has retained the tense of the original direct speech rather than following the rules of sequence (see Chapter 17 note).

dum . . . ludificetur – subjunctive either because this is a subordinate clause in Oratio Obliqua, or because the subjunctive is a mood often used by Tacitus in temporal clauses.

invalida et inermia – in apposition to *patres et plebem*; the neuter gender is used to denote these two classes viewed as a whole rather than any particular individuals.

cunctatione ficta – see Tacitus' account of the start of Tiberius' principate (Chapters 11–13).

miles – the singular noun is used collectively.

adulescentium – there is an exaggeration here; Germanicus was twenty-nine, Drusus twenty-seven.

auctoritate – see Introduction, p.3: no matter what *imperium* Drusus/ Germanicus brought with them, their youth limited their natural influence over the troops.

ire ipsum . . . debuisse – accusative and infinitive as a main clause statement within Oratio Obliqua: 'he should have gone in person.'

maiestatem imperatoriam – *maiestas* means 'greatness' or 'dignity'. The reference is to Tiberius' superior standing both in his role as *princeps*, but also because of his previous military successes as the commander (*imperator*) of troops in Germany and Illyria (see Introduction, p.8).

cessuris – 'likely to yield'. The future participle often carries this sense.

longa experientia – descriptive ablative.

eundem . . . summum – 'the same man the utmost . . . ', i.e., 'and in one and the same man the height of severity and generosity'. As *princeps*, Tiberius had the power to inflict the most severe punishments and grant the most generous largesse.

an – *an* introduces a tone of surprise; the implication is that if Augustus managed to visit the troops, so too should Tiberius.

fessa aetate – descriptive ablative – 'with wearisome old-age', i.e., 'exhausted by age'. In fact, Augustus spent time with the German legions between 16–13 BC when he has between forty-seven and fifty years old; in AD 14, Tiberius was fifty-six.

vigentem annis – 'strong in years' (see note above).

satis prospectum – understand *esse* – 'enough thought had been given . . . '.

adhibenda – understand *esse*.

ferre pacem – 'to put up with peace', i.e., the soldiers had mutinied because they were not distracted by the demands of an active campaign; they needed to learn to accept the conditions of military service even without the threat of imminent death in battle or the prospect of the rewards of victory.

Chapter 47

immotum . . . fixumque Tiberio fuit – the subject of *fuit* is *non omittere . . . neque dare*; in English this is best translated as 'the resolve not to abandon . . . nor to hand over . . . was immovable and fixed for Tiberius'.

A Level

in casum dare – i.e., without his presence to direct affairs they would all be subject to the whims of chance; Tiberius' power over Rome is presented as total.

quippe – here used corroboratively – 'and what's more'.

validior . . . exercitus – understand *erat*; notice that Tiberius' thoughts are given the immediacy of direct speech.

subnixus – 'was supported by'. In the context of recent Civil Wars, Tiberius' fear is the risk these legions – if disloyal – might pose to Rome itself: the German legions were far enough away to be able to separate themselves from Rome altogether because their supplies came from Gaul. The Pannonian legions, in contrast, were close enough to be an immediate threat to Italy.

quos ... anteferret – the subjunctive is deliberative, i.e., the implication is that this is question that cannot be answered.

ac ne ... incenderentur – an introductory verb needs to be understood – 'and he was afraid that . . .'.

adiri – the syntax has shifted to Oratio Obliqua; this infinitive is used impersonally (see Chapter 17 note) – 'there was an equal approach', i.e., the legions could be handled in a way which did not prioritise one over the other.

maiestate salva – 'with his own status intact' – i.e., there would be no risk that his own dignity would be reduced by an unsuccessful meeting with the legions.

cui – possessive dative – 'for which there was . . .'.

excusatum – 'it was excusable'.

resistentes – the accusative subject of *posse*.

quod aliud subsidium – understand *fore* (the question is rhetorical and so takes the accusative and infinitive construction in Oratio Obliqua).

si ... sprevissent – the pluperfect subjunctive represents the future perfect indicative in the original direct speech conditional clause (see *The Oxford Latin Grammar*, pp.86–87).

ut iam iamque iturus – 'as if at any moment about to leave'. *iam iamque* is emphatic, and gives the impression of a repeated façade (see the start of Chapter 46 – *Immotum ... fixumque*).

varie causatus – 'having given the different reasons of ....'.

primo ... dein ... diutissime – *primo* and *dein* do not mean that he fooled one, then the other, but instead that he fooled the sensible for least long, the mob in Rome for longer, and the provincials for longest of all.

Chapter 48

si ... sibi ipsi consulerent – 'to see if they might take thought in their own interest', i.e., Germanicus wished to wait in the hope that the soldiers would regret their actions and no longer need him to intervene.

recenti exemplo – i.e., what had happened to the other legions (see Chapter 44).

Caecinam – after taking the I and XX legions to Colonia (Cologne) (see Chapter 37), Caecina must have returned to the V and XXI legions at Vetera (Xanten).

venire se – Oratio Obliqua to report the contents of the letter.

A
Level

ni ... praesumant – this present subjunctive represents the future simple of the original direct speech; the present tense is because the leading verb (*praemittit*) is historic present, and so can be treated vividly as primary sequence (see *The Oxford Latin Grammar*, pp.86–87)

quod maxime castrorum sincerum erat – the omitted antecedent for this clause is the third indirect object of *recitat*; *quod* is neuter because it refers to a category rather than an individual: 'he read the letter in secret to the eagle-bearers, the standard-bearers, and to the most trustworthy members of the camp.' After the centurions, the *aquiliferi* and the *signiferi* were the next most senior; in the absence of the centurions (for their death or flight see Chapter 32), these men were the obvious deputies.

eximant – in Silver Latin, *eximo* is regularly followed by an accusative and a dative; in Classical Latin, the dative after *eximo* is typically for persons, but by this time it is used for both persons and things.

nam ... cadere: Oratio Obliqua – Caecina's speech continues.

temptatis – ablative absolute; the noun described is the antecedent to *quos*.

postquam ... vident – the historic present tense continues.

de sententia legati – 'in accordance with the legate's plan.'

quo ... invadant – *quo* is temporal – 'at which' – and the subjunctive *invadant* shows this to be purpose clause.

foedissimum quemque – superlative + *quisque* – 'all the most shameful' (see Chapter 16 note).

nisi consciis – *consciis* is ablative because it is part of the ablative absolute.

quod ... quis ... – both are interrogative.

A Level

Chapter 49

omnium ... civilium armorum – the genitive is to be translated with *facies* – 'the appearance of all civil wars' – this is quite clearly not a civil war, and so an exaggeration by Tacitus, but the choice of words reminds the reader that these are Romans killed by Romans, and it sets the aftermath of this mutiny amid all the horror of the years of recent civil war.

accidere – the abbreviated form of *acciderunt*.

quos – the antecedent (omitted) is the subject of *discedunt* and needs to be supplied in English: 'men who ...'.

simul vescentes ... simul quietos ... – 'eating together ... at rest together'; *simul* highlights the previous unity of the troops.

in partes – 'to different sides'.

clamor vulnera sanguis ... – understand *erant*.

caesi – understand *sunt*.

intellecto – impersonal ablative absolute – 'once it was understood ...'.

saeviretur – the impersonal construction (see Chapter 17 note) – 'against whom the savagery was directed'.

moderator adfuit – *moderator* is the complement – 'neither *legatus* nor *tribunus* was there to restrain them'.

permissa – understand *est. licentia, ultio* and *satietas* are all subjects, but *permissa* is singular with the nearest subject. All three subjects are connected (i.e., the freedom to take their fill of revenge); Tacitus presents them separately to ensure equal weight and emphasis for each.

non medicinam . . . sed cladem – notice that *plurimis cum lacrimis* disrupts the natural word order and gains emphasis accordingly.

cupido . . . eundi – the genitive is the usual case for a gerund which follows another noun – 'the desire to go . . .'.

piaculum furoris – *piaculum* is in apposition to their wish – 'as an expiation of their madness'.

nec . . . posse placari . . . manes – accusative and infinitive for Oratio Obliqua to report the wish of the troops.

accepissent – the pluperfect subjunctive represents the future perfect indicative of the original direct speech conditional clause (see *The Oxford Latin Grammar*, pp.86–87).

quarum – i.e., the auxiliary cohorts and the cavalry.

modestia – 'restraint' and so 'discipline'.

Vocabulary

An asterisk * denotes a word in OCR's Defined Vocabulary List for AS.

*a, ab	by, from
abdo, abdere, abdidi, abditum	to hide away
abicio, abicere, abieci, abiectum	to throw away
abnuo -nuere -nui -nuitum	to refuse, deny
aboleo -olere -olevi -olitum	to wipe away
abscedo -cedere -cessi -cessum	to leave
abstrusus -a -um	secret, hard to fathom
*absum, abesse, afui	to be away from
*ac	and
accedo -cedere -cessi -cessum	to approach
accendo, accendere, accendi, accensum	to inflame (*metaphorically* – to enrage)
*accido, accidere, accidi	to happen
accio, accire, accivi, accitum	to summon
*accipio, accipere, accepi, acceptum	to receive
*acer, acris, acre	sharp, keen
Actiacus -a -um	relating to the Battle of Actium
*ad	to, towards, for the purpose of
adcelero -are	to hasten
adclamo -are	shout approval
adcresco -crescere -crevi -cretum	to grow, rise
adcurro -currere -curri -cursum	to run to
adcursus -us, m	onrush
additus -us, m	addition
*addo, addere, addidi, additum	to add
*adeo	so greatly, to such an extent
adeo, adire, adii, aditum	to approach
adfero, adferre, attuli, adlatum	to bring to, announce
adficio -ficere -feci -fectum	to affect by, treat with, to work upon
adhibeo -ere	to apply
*adhuc	still
adicio -icere -ieci -iectum	to apply, to put upon
*adipiscor, adipisci, adeptus sum	to acquire, obtain

adlevo -are	to relieve, reduce, to lift up
admodum	completely, very much a
admoneo -ere	to remind
adoptio -onis, f	adoption
adorno -are	to prepare, furnish
adpono -ponere -posui -positum	to put in charge (+ dat), appoint
adscio -scire	to take to oneself, to adopt
adscribo -scribere -scripsi -scriptum	to write in
adsimulo -are	to liken
adsoleo -ere	to be accustomed
adstrepo -ere	to applaud, shout approval
adsuetudo -inis, f	habit
adsum, adesse, adfui	to be present, to be at hand
adsumo -sumere -sumpsi -sumptum	to take on, receive, adopt
adulatio -onis, f	praise, flattery
***adulescens -entis**	adolescent, young, young man
adultus -a -um	adult
***advenio -venire -veni -ventum**	to arrive
adventus -us, m	arrival
adversor -ari (+ dat)	to oppose
***adversus -a -um**	opposing, against, towards
advolvo -volvere -volvi -volutum	to throw oneself at the feet of, to roll to
aeger, aegra, aegrum	ill
aegre	with difficulty
aemulatio -onis, f	rivalry, jealousy
aequalitas -atis, f	equality
aes, aeris, n	bronze
aestas -atis, f	summer
aestimo -are	to value
aestiva -orum, n pl	summer camp
aestivus -a -um	of summer
aetas, aetatis, f	age, prime of life
aeternus -a -um	ever-lasting, eternal
***ager, agri, m**	fields (i.e. land suitable for farming), land
aggero -gerere -gessi -gessum	to bring to
agito -are	to be engaged upon, discuss, agitate, consider
***agmen, agminis, n**	marching column, column of men

*ago, agere, egi, actum	to act, take action, do, drive
aio, ait (*defective verb*)	to say
ala -ae, f	cavalry division
*alii . . . alii	some . . . others
alio	elsewhere, to another place
*aliquis, aliquid	someone, something, anyone, anything
*aliter	otherwise
*alius -a -ud	other, another
*alter, altera, alterum	other (of two), another
ambigo, ambigere	to be unsure
ambiguus -a -um	ambiguous, unsure
ambitus -us, m	canvassing, ambition
*ambulo -are	to walk
amici -orum, m pl	(pl) entourage
*amicus -i, m	friend
*amitto -mittere -misi -missum	to lose
*amor, amoris, m	love
an	*introduces a question*
*an	or, whether
ango, angere, anxi, anctum	to hurt, distress, throttle, torment
anima -ae, f	soul
*animus -i, m	mind, spirit, heart
annona -ae, f	food-suply, corn
*annus -i, m	year
*ante (+ acc)	before
*antea	before
antefero -ferre -tuli -latum	to prefer
antiquus -a -um	old-school
anxius -a -um	concerned
*aperio, aperire, aperui, apertum	to reveal, disclose
appello -are	to call, name
*apud, aput (+ acc)	in the presence of, among
apud Rhenum	on the Rhine
apud senatum	before the Senate
apud urbem	in the city
*aquila -ae, f	eagle, legionary standard (i.e. the emblem of the legion)
aquilifer -feri, m	eagle-bearer
*ara -ae, f	altar, monument

arbiter -tri, m	arbitrator, judge
arbitrium -i, n	will, decision
arcanus -a um	secret
ardor, ardoris, m	passion, eagerness
arduus -a -um	steep, difficult
arguo, arguere, argui, argutum	to prove
*arma -orum, n pl	military equipment, weapons
armati -orum, m pl	armed men
Armenia -ae, f	Armenia
armo -are	to arm
*ars, artis, f	art, skill, attribute, strategem, trick
as, assis, m	as (Roman coin)
aspecto -are	to keep looking at earnestly
asper, aspera, asperum	harsh
aspernor -ari	to reject, spurn, scorn, despise
aspicio, aspicere, aspexi, aspectum	look at, see
*at	but
at hercule	By Hercules!
*atque	and
atrox, atrocis	fierce, savage, spirited
auctor -oris, m	leader, instigator, author
auctoritas -atis, f	influence, authority
*audeo, audere, ausus sum	to dare
*audio, audire, audivi, auditum	I hear
*aufero, auferre, abstuli, ablatum	to remove
*augeo, augere, auxi, auctum	to increase, bolster
aula -ae, f	palace
auris, auris, f	ear
*aut	or
*auxilia -orum, n pl	auxiliary forces
aversor -ari	to turn away from
avidus -a -um	eager
avus -i, m	grandfather
*bellum -i, n	war
*bene	well
bini -ae -a	two (each)
*bonus -a -um	good, noble

cadaver -eris, n	corpse
*cado, cadere, cecidi, casum	to fall
*caedes -is, f	slaughter, murder, death
caedo, caedere, cecidi, caesum	to slaughter, kill
caelestis -e	celestial
*caelum -i, n	sky, heavens
Caesar, Caesaris, m	family name for the *gens Iulia* (Julius Caesar in particular), and then subsequently for the Princeps and his sons
caespes -itis, m	turf
candidatus -i, m	candidate
canities -ei, f	grey hair
capax, capacis	capable, fit for
capesso -ere -ivi -itum	to seize eagerly, grab hold of
*caput, capitis, n	head
carcer, carceris, m	prison
caritas -atis, f	affection
*castra -orum, n pl	camp
casus -us, m	chance, fortune, misfortune
casu	by chance
*causa -ae, f	cause, reason
causa (+gen)	for the sake of
causor -ari	to give as a reason
cavillor -ari	to joke, jeer
*cedo, cedere, cessi, cessum	to turn out, yield, withdraw
cedo	Give!
censeo, censere, censui, censum	to vote, recommend, express an opinion
centuria -ae, f	century (section of the army)
*centurio -onis, m	centurion (60 in a legion)
*certamen, certaminis, n	struggle, contest
certo -are	to battle it out
*certus -a -um	fixed, certain
*ceteri -ae -a	others, the rest
ceterum	but, meanwhile, however
*ceterus -a -um	the rest of
cieo, ciere, civi, citum	to move, incite, to utter
circumeo -ire -ii -itum	to go around

circumicio -icere -ieci -iectum	to surround
circumsisto -sistere -steti	to stand around, to stand by
circumsto -stare -steti	to stand around, to surround
circumvenio -venire -veni -ventum	surround
civilis -e	civil, belonging to a citizen
*civis -is, m	citizen
*civitas -atis, f	city-state, group of citizens
*clades -is, f	disaster
clamito -are	to keep shouting
*clamor, clamoris, m	shout, shouting
claritudo -inis, f	brightness
*clarus -a -um	brilliant, clear, loud
classis, classis, f	fleet
claudo, claudere, clausi, clausum	to shut up
codicilli -orum, m	letter, note
*coepi, coepisse, coeptum	to begin
coerceo -cere -cui -citum	to enclose
coetus -us, i	crowd
cognomentum -i, n	name
*cognosco, cognoscere, cognovi, cognitum	to find out
*cohors, cohortis, f	cohort, retinue
collega -ae, m	colleague, partner in office
colligo, colligere, collegi, collectum	to gather, collect
*comes, comitis, c	companion
comitas -atis, f	friendliness
comitor -ari	to accompany
commeo -are	to visit frequently
commilito -onis, m	fellow-soldier
commodum -n, n	advantage, benefit
commoveo -movere -movi -motum	to move, excite
communis -e	common, shared
comperio -perire -peri -pertum	to discover, find out, to discover (guilty)
compono -ponere -posui -positum	to compose, arrange
comprimo -primere -pressi -pressum	to suppress, restrain
concedo -cedere -cessi -cessum	to withdraw, to grant, allow, assent to
concentus -us, m	a singing together, unison

concieo -ciere -civi -citum	to stir up, excite, assemble
condicio -onis, f	condition, terms
condo, condere, condidi, conditum	to bury, hide
confessio -onis, f	admission
***conficio -ficere -feci -fectum**	to complete
congero -gerere -gessi -gestum	to heap up, pile up
congrego – are	to flock together, gather
coniecto -are	to guess
conloquium -i, n	conversation
conquiro -quirere -quisivi -quisitum	to gather together, search for
conscius -a -um	confidant, witness
consentio -sentire -sensi -sensum	to agree
consido -sidere -sedi -sessum	to settle
***consilium -i, n**	advice, plan
consors, consortis	having an equal share in
conspicuus -a -um	obvious, striking
consternatio -onis, f	dismay, tumult
consto, constare, constiti, constatum	to agree
constat	it is agreed, well known
***consul, consulis, m**	consul
consulatus -us, m	consulship
consulo -sulere -sului -sultum (+ dat)	to consult, deliberate; (+ dat) to take thought for
consultum -i, n	decree, plan
contemno -temnere -tempsi -temptum	to scorn, despise
contineo -tinere -tinui -tentum	to contain
continuus -a -um	incessant, continuous
contio -onis, f	assembly, meeting
contionabundus -a -um	harranging (a political assembly)
***contra (+ acc)**	contrary to
contraho -trahere -traxi -tractum	to gather together, unite
contubernium -i, n	tent
contumacia -ae, f	arrogance, obstinacy
contumelia -ae, f	insult
convello – vellere -velli -vulsum	to tear up, wrench away
coram (+ acc)	in the presence of
cornu -us, n	horn

*corpus -oris, n	body
credibilis -e	plausible, credible
*credo, credere, credidi, creditum	to believe
cremo -are	to cremate
*crimen -inis, n	accusation, crime, guilt
cruciatus -us, m	torture
cruentus -a -um	bloodied
cubile -is, n	resting place
*culpa -ae, f	fault, blame
*cum	when, since, although
*cum (+ abl)	with
cumulo -are	to pile up
cunctabundus -a -um	hesitant
cunctatio -onis, f	delay, hesitation
cunctor -ari	to hesitate
*cunctus -a -um	all
cupido, cupidinis, f	desire
*cupio, cupere, cupivi, cupitum	to desire, with
*cur	why
*cura -ae, f	concern, care, responsibility
curatus -a -um	urgent, matter of concern
curia -ae, f	Senate-house
curulis -is, f	curule chair
curuli aedilitate	an aedile's curule chair
custodia -ae, f	guard (collective noun)
*custos, custodis, m	guard
damno -are	to condemn
*de (+ abl)	about, concerning, for the reason of, down from, from
*dea -ae, f	goddess
*debeo, debere, debui, debitum	to owe, ought
decerno -cernere -crevi -cretum	to decide, choose
decorus -a -um	seemly, fit
defectio -onis, f	failiure
defector -oris, m	rebel
defero -ferre -tuli -latum	to defer, bring down, report
deformis -e	ugly, shameful
defungor -fungi -functus sum	to finish with, die

*dein	then
deligo -ligere -legi -lectum	to choose
deminutio -onis, f	lessening, diminution
denarius -i, m	denarius (Roman coin)
deni -ae -a	10 (each)
*denique	in short, finally
depello -pellere -puli -pulsum	to divert
deposco -poscere -poposci	to demand
deprecor -ari	to beg (for mercy), apologize
deripio -ripere -ripui -reptum	to pull down
desciso -sciscere -scivi -scitum	to revolt from
desero -serere -serui -sertum	to abandon, desert
desertor -oris, m	deserter
desiderium -i, n	wish, desire, request
designatus consul	consul designate (i.e. the next man to hold the consulship)
*desino -sinere -sii -situm	to cease
desolo -are	to abandon
destino -are	to designate
detero -terere -trivi -tritum	to wear out
deterrimus -a -um	worst
detorqueo -torquere -torsi -tortum	to distort
*deus -i, m	god
devincio -vincire -vinxi -vinctum	to bind, tie fast
*dico, dicere, dixi, dictum	to say
dictito -are	to say repeatedly
*dies -ei, m	day
differo, differre, distuli, dilatum	to scatter, spread, discredit
*dignitas -atis, f	dignity
*dignus -a -um (+ abl)	worthy
digredior -gredi -gressus sum	to go away from
dilabor -labi -lapsus sum	to slip away, disperse
dimitto -mittere -misi -missum	to discharge, dismiss
diripio -ripere -ripui -reptum	to fling aside, to divide as spoil, ransack, plunder
*discedo -cedere -cessi -cessum	to go apart
discessio -onis, f	departure

disciplina -ae, f	military discipline
***disco, discere, didici**	to learn
discordia -ae, f	discord, strife
discordo -are	to be mutinous
discrepo -are -ui	to differ, disagree
disicio -icere -ieci -iectum	to cast aside
dissero, disserere, disserui,	to discuss
dissertum	
dissideo -sidere -sedi -sessum	to disagree, to be opposed
dissocio -are	to separate from
distraho -trahere -traxi -tractum	to pull apart
***diu**	for a long time
diurnus -a -um	a day's
***diutissime**	for a very long time
diversus -a -um	different
***dives -itis**	rich
***divido -videre -visi -visum**	to divide
divus -a -um	deified, divine
***do, dare, dedi, datum**	to give
***doceo, docere, docui, doctum**	to teach
documentum -i, n	proof
***dolor, doloris, m**	pain, grief
***dolus -i, m**	subterfuge, trickery
dominatio -onis, f	domination, despotisim
***dominus -i, m**	master
***domus -us, f**	home, house, household, family
***domi**	at home
donec	until
dubitatio -onis, f	hestitation
dubium -i, n	doubt
dubium an	perhaps
***duco, ducere, duxi, ductum**	to lead
ducere in matrimonium	to marry
***dum**	so long as, while
***duo -ae -o**	two
***duodecim**	twelve
duro -are	to harden, to continue
***durus -a -um**	harsh
***dux, ducis, m**	leader

*e, ex (+ abl)	out of, from, arising from
edictum -i, n	edict
educo -ducere -duxi -ductum	to bring up
effero, efferre, extuli, elatum	to promote, raise, exalt
effigies -ei, f	statue, image
effringo -fringere -fregi -fractum	to break open
effundo -fundere -fudi -fusum	to pour forth
*ego, me, mei, mihi, me	I, me
*egredior -gredi -gressus sum	to go out from
egregie	with distinction, outstandingly
egregius -a -um	excellent
eligo -ligere -legi -lectum	to choose, elect
emeritus -i, m	a soldier who has served his time, a veteran
enimvero	indeed, what's more
*eo	to that point, for that reason
*eo, ire, ivi, itum	to go
*epistula -ae, f	letter
*eques, equitis, m	*eques* (i.e. a man of equestrian rank), equestrian
*ergo	therefore
erumpo, erumpere, erupi, eruptum	to burst forth, erupt into
*et	and, also, even
etenim	for
*etiam	even, also
evito -are	to avoid
exanimis -e	unconscious
excedo -cedere -cessi -cessum	to die, to depart, to go beyond
excessus -us, m	death
*excipio -cipere -cepi -ceptum	to receive, listen to
excubiae -arum, f	guard, guard-duties
excuso -are	to excuse
*exemplum -i, n	example
*exercitus -us, m	army
*exilium -i, n	exile, banishment
eximo -imere -emi -emptum	to remove from, to free
*exitium -i, n	death, destruction
exitus -us, m	outcome, death
experientia -ae, f	experience

experior, experiri, expertus sum	to experience
expers, expertis (+ gen)	devoid of, without
expleo -plere -plevi -pletum	to complete
exposco -poscere -poposci	to demand
expostulatio -onis, f	demand
expostulo -are	to demand
exprimo -primere -pressi -pressum	to force out, extort
exprobro -are	to lay to the charge of, criticize
exsequor -sequi -secutus sum	to accomplish
***exspecto -are**	to wait for
exstruo -struere -struxi -structum	to construct
extinguo, extinguere, exstinxi, exstinctum	to extinguish, kill
***extra (+ acc)**	beyond, outside
extrudo -trudere -trusi -trusum	to push out
exul, exulis, c	exile
exuo, exuere, exui, exutum	cast off
facetia -ae, f	wit, facetiousness
facies -ei, f	appearance
***facilis -e**	easy
***facinus -oris, n**	crime, deed
***facio, facere, feci, factum**	to make, do
factum -i, n	deed
***fallo, fallere, fefelli, falsum**	to deceive
falsus -a -um	false
***fama -ae, f**	rumour, reputation
***familia -ae, f**	family, household
fas (indeclinable)	divine law
fastigium -i, n	pediment of a roof, high rank, dignity
fateor, fateri, fassus sum	to admit, acknowledge
fatigo -are	to tire, wear out
fatum -i, n	fate
favor -oris, m	popularity
***femina -ae, f**	woman
***fero, ferre, tuli, latum**	to bring, support, carry, bear, put up with, endure
ferocia -ae, f	arrogance, courage

*ferox, ferocis	fierce, over-confident, savage
*ferrum -i, n	iron, sword
fessus -a -um	tired, worn out
*festino -are	to hurry, hasten
fictus -a -um	fictitious, false
*fides -ei, f	loyalty, trustworthiness
*filia -ae, f	daughter
*filius -i, m	son
filios familiarum	minors (i.e. those still under the jurisdiction of their fathers)
finio -ire	to finish
*finis, finis, m	end, death
firmatus -a -um	resolute
firmo -are	strengthen
fixus -a -um	fixed
flagitium -i, n	shameful/disgraceful behaviour, disgrace
flagrans -antis	blazing, passionate
flagrantissime	most ardently
flecto, flectere, flexi, flectum	to bend
fletus -us, m	weeping
*foedus -a -um	shameful, base
fomentum -i, n	remedy, poultice
formido -inis, f	fear
fors, fortis, f	chance, fortune
forte	by chance
*fortis -e	tough, brave, strong
*fortuna -ae, f	fortune
*forum -i, n	forum
*frango, frangere, fregi, fractum	to break
*frater, fratris, m	brother
*frustra	in vain, to no purpose
frustror -ari	to disappoint, deceive
*fugio, fugere, fugi, fugitum	to flee
fulgeo, fulgere, fulsi	to gleam, glitter
fulgor -oris, m	brilliance, splendour
fungor, fungi, functus sum	to perform, carry out
funus -eris, n	funeral
*furor -oris, m	madness, anger, frenzy

*Gallia -ae, f	Gaul (NB there were two Gauls – Cisalpine (equivalent to Northern Italy) and Transalpine (equivalent to France)
*gaudium -i, n	joy
gemino -are	to double
gemitus -us, m	groan
gener, generi, m	son-in-law
genitus -a -um	born
*gens, gentis, f	race, tribe
genu -us, n	knee
*Germani -orum, m pl	the Germans
*Germania -ae, f	Germany
*Germanicus -a -um	relating to Germany
gladiator -oris, m	gladiators
globus – i, m	ball, mass, crowd
gloria -ae, f	glory
gnarus -a -um	known, knowing
*gratia -ae, f	indulgence, thanks, favour
gratus -a -um	pleasing
gravesco, gravescere	to grow ill, grow worse
*gravis -e	burdensome
gravo -are	to weigh down
gregarius -a -um	common, low level
*habeo, habere, habui, habitum	I have, hold, keep, consider
*haud	not
hebesco -ere	to grow blunt, grow faint
hercule	By Hercules!
hiberna -orum, n pl	winter-quarters
*hic	here
*hic, haec, hoc	this
*hiems, hiemis, f	winter
*hinc	from here, after this
Hispaniensis -e	Spanish
histrionalis -e	belong to an actor
honestus -a -um	honourable
*honor -oris, m	distinction, honour, public office
horridus -a -um	savage, wild

hortatus -us, m	encouragement
*hortor -ari	to encourage, urge
*hostis, hostis, m	enemy
*iacio, iacere, ieci, iactum	to throw, mention
*iam	already, now
ictus -us, m	blow
idcirco	for that reason
*idem, eadem, idem	the same
ideo	therefore, on that account
*idoneus -a -um	suitable
*igitur	therefore
ignarus -a -um	unaware
ignobilis -e	ignoble
ignominia -ae, f	dishonour
*ille, illa, illud	that
*illic	in that place, there
illuc	thither, to that place
Illyricum -i, n	Illyricum
imber, imbris, m	rain
imbuo, imbuere, imbui, imbutum	to soak, stain
imitor -ari	to imitate
immensus -a -um	big, great, huge
immotus -a -um	immoveable, unmoved, motionless
impedimenta -orum, n pl	baggage
*imperator -oris, m	(military) commander, the *princeps* (in his role as overall commander of the army)
imperatorius -a -um	belonging to an *imperator*
*imperium -i, n	right of command, order, empire
proconsulare imperium	imperium equal to a proconsul
*impero -are	to rule, command, order
impius -a -um	impious, wicked
impleo, implere, implevi, impletum	to fill, sate
implico -are	to entangle
impune	with impunity
*in (+ abl)	in, on

*in (+ acc)	into, towards, against, for the purpose of
in cassum	in vain
in praesens	for the moment
in universum	altogether
incedo -cedere -cessi -cessum	to proceed, advance, come (up) on
*incendo -cendere -cendi -censum	to inflame, anger
inceptum -i, n	enterprise, undertaking
incertus -a -um	uncertain
*incipio -cipere -cepi -ceptum	to begin
incitamentum -i, n	incentive
inclinatio -onis, f	inclination
incolumis -e	unharmed
increpo -are	to speak loudly, rebuke
incultus -a -um	wild, uncultivated
incuso -are	to accuse, blame
*inde	then
indicium -i, n	indication
indico -dicere -dixi -dictum	to declare
indignus -a -um	unworthy
indo -dere -didi -ditum	to give as a name
induco -ducere -duxi -ductum	to bring in/into
ineo -ire -ii -itum	to start upon, begin
inermis -e	unarmed
inertia -ae, f	inertia, idleness
infamia -ae, f	shame, disgrace
infantia -ae, f	infancy
infaustus -a -um	unlucky
infensus -a -um	hostile
*infero, inferre, intuli, inlatum	to put on, to bring on
infirmus -a -um	lowest
infringo -fringere -fregi -fractum	to break
infructuosus -a -um	unprofitable
ingenitus -a -um	innate
*ingenium -i, n	intellect, character, talent
*ingens, ingentis	huge
ingero -gerere -gessi -gestum	to throw upon, to heap upon
*ingredior -gredi -gressus sum	to enter
ingruo, ingruere, ingrui	to fall upon, attack

*initium -i, n	beginning
inlustris -e	famous, bright
inluvies -ei, f	dirt, mud
inmineo -ere	to threaten
inmitis -e	harsh, cruel
innocens -entis	innocent
inpar, inparis	unequal
inpeditus -a -um	impeded, obstructed, difficult
inpello -pellere -puli -pulsum	to break into, incite
inplacabilis -e	implacable
inpono -ponere -posui -positum	to put in charge of
inpotentia -ae, f	lack of restraint, violent passion
inprovisus -a -um	unforeseen, unexpected
inquit	he/she/it said
inrepo -repere -repsi -reptum	to crawl in
inrisus -us, m	mockery
inritus -a -um	in vain
*inrumpo -rumpere -rupi -ruptum	to burst into
insector -ari	to chase after, harry
insero -serere -serui -sertum	to put in, insert
insignia -um, n pl	military decorations
insisto -sistere -stiti	to stand firm within
insitus -a -um	ingrained
instar (+ gen)	equal to
*insula -ae, f	island
insuper	in addition
integer, integra, integrum	intact, whole
intellego -legere -lexi -lectum	to understand
intemeratus -a -um	undefiled
intendo -tendere -tendi -tentum	to stretch, direct
intento -are	to stretch out threateningly
intentus -a -um	strict, eager, intent on
*inter (+ acc)	among, between
intercedo -cedere -cessi -cessum	to veto
interdum	from time to time, sometimes
*interea	meanwhile
*interficio -ficere -feci -fectum	to kill
intericio -icere -ieci -iectum	to interpose, to intervene with
*interim	meanwhile, for the time being

intermitto – mittere -misi -missum	to leave off, interrupt, pause
interrogatio -onis, f	question
interrogo -are	to ask
interrumpo -rumpere -rupi - **ruptum**	to interrupt, pause
*intra (+ acc)	within
introeo -ire -ii -itum	to enter
introspicio -spicere -spexi **-spectum**	to look into
invado -vadere -vasi -vasum	to attack, invade
invalidus -a -um	weak
invehor -vehi – vectus sum	to attack with words
invideo -videre -vidi -visum	to begrudge
invidia -ae, f	ill-will, jealousy
invisus -a -um	hated
involo -are	to fly at, pounce upon, seize
*ipse, ipsa, ipsum	himself, herself, itself, themselves
*ira -ae, f	anger
irascor, irasci, iratus sum	to be angry
*is, ea, id	he, she, it, this, that
*ita	thus
*Italia -ae, f	Italy
*iter, itineris, n	road, journey
*iubeo, iubere, iussi, iussum	to order
iugulo -are	to cut the throat of
*iungo, iungere, iunxi, iunctum	to join, connect
iunior -oris, m	younger man
iuro -are	to swear (an oath)
ius, iuris, n	right, oath, authority
iussum -i, n	order
iustitium -i, n	a pause in public business, period of public mourning
*iuvenis -is, m	young man
iuventus -utis, f	youth, young people
iuxta	near by, side by side
labor -oris, m	hard work, toil
lacrima -ae, f	tear
laetor -ari	to be happy, rejoice

*laetus -a -um	happy
lamentor -ari	to lament, bewail
languesco -ere, langui	to grow faint
lapis, lapidis, m	stone
largior -iri	to bestow lavishly
largitio -onis, f	gift, largess, bribery
lascivio -ire	to be wanton, run riot
latebrae -arum, f	hiding-places
*laus, laudis, f	praise
legatio -onis, f	embassy
*legatus -i, m	deputy, legionary commander, envoy
*legio, legionis, f	legion
*lego, legere, legi, lectum	to choose
lenio, lenire	to soothe
levamentum -i, n	alleviation, remedy
*levis -e	light
*lex, legis (f)	law, condition, terms
libellum -i, n	little book, document, pamphlet
*libenter	willingly
*libertas -atis, f	liberty, political freedom
libido -inis, f	passion, sexual desire
licentia -ae, f	freedom, power, lack of restraint, licentiousness
lictor -oris, m	lictor (an attendant to a senior magistrate)
lingua -ae, f	speech, language
*linquo, linqere, liqui	to leave
*litterae -as, f pl	letter
loco -are	to place, put
*locus -i, m	place, position, origin (= birth)
longinquus -a -um	far away
*longus -a -um	long
*loquor, loqui, locutus sum	to speak
luctus -us, m	grief
ludibrium -i, n	insult
ludificor -ari	to make a game of, delude
luna -ae, f	moon
*lux, lucis, f	light, life
luxus -us, m	luxury, excess

maereo -ere	to be sad
maestitia -ae, f	sorrow, grief
*magis	more
magistratus -us, m	political office, magistracy, magistrate
magnitudo -inis, f	greatness
*magnus -a -um	large, great
maiestas -atis, f	greatness, dignity, majesty
*malo, malle, malui	to prefer
malum -i, n	trouble, wrong
*malus -a -um	wicked, a wrong-doer
mandata -orum, n pl	instructions, orders, commands
*mando -are	to entrust, to give orders to
manes -ium, m pl	shades (spirit of the dead)
manipularis -e	*manipularis* (i.e. a soldier in a maniple)
manipulus -i, m	maniple (a group of foot-soldiers)
*manus -us, m	hand, band of men
maritus -i, m	husband
*mater, matris, f	mother
maturus -a -um	advanced, mature
*maxime	especially
*maximus -a -um	greatest
medicina -ae, f	medicine, remedy
meditor -ari	to think over, consider
melior, melius	better
*mens, mentis, f	mind
*mensis -is, m	month
mereo, merere, merui, meritum	to earn, deserve
mereor, mereri	to earn, deserve
meritum -i, n	merit
*metus -us, m	fear
metuo, metuere, metui, metutum	to fear
*meus -a -um	my
*miles, militis, m	soldier, soldiers (collective noun)
militaris -e	belonging to a soldier, military
militia -ae, f	military service
*mille, milia	thousand
minae -arum, f pl	threats
minax, minacis	menacing
minister, ministri, m	agent, participant, helper

ministerium -i, n	task, assistance
*minor, minus	lesser, inferior
mirus -a -um	remarkable, astonishing
misceo, miscere, miscui, mixtum	to mix, combine, stir up
*miser -a -um	wretched
misericordia -ae, f	pity
missio -onis, f	discharge
mitigo -are	to soften, appease
*mitto, mittere, misi, missum	to send
mobilis -e	susceptible, easily moved
moderator -oris, m	controller
moderor -ari	to keep moderate, restrain
modestia -ae, f	restraint, diffidence, moderation, good conduct
modicus -a -um	moderate, limited
*modo	only
*modus -i, m	measure, manner, way, sort/kind
moles -is, f	burden, task
*moneo, monere	to advise, warn
*mons, montis, m	mountain
*mors, mortis, f	death
*mos, moris, m	custom, habit, political constitution
*mores	character
motus -us, m	movement, movement of the mind, emotion, uprising
*mox	soon
muliebris -e	belonging to a woman
*multitudo -inis, f	crowd
multo	by far
*multus -a -um	much, (pl) many
municipium -i, n	town
munificientia -ae, f	generosity
munimentum -i, n	defence, protection
*munus -eris, n	duty
murmur, murmuris, n	murmur, grumbling
*muto, mutare	I change
*nam	for
-nam	*emphatic particle*

natura -ae, f	nature
***natus -a -um**	born
Nauportum -i, n	Nauportum
***navis -is, f**	ship
***ne**	not to, in order not to, that ... (not)
ne ... quidem	not even
***-ne**	*denotes a question*
***nec**	and not, nor
necdum	not yet
necessitas -atis, f	necessity
***nego -are**	to deny, refuse
***negotium -i, n**	business
nepos, nepotis, m	grandson
nequaquam	in no way
***neque ... neque**	neither ... nor
nequeo, nequire, nequii, nequitum	not to be able
neu	nor, neither
nex, necis, f	death, murder
ni	if not, unless
***nihil**	nothing
nihilo minus	nevertheless
***nisi**	if not, except, unless
nitor, niti, nisus sum	to strive
nobilitas -atis, f	nobility
nocturnus -a -um	at night, nocturnal
Nola -ae, f	Nola
***nomen, nominis, n**	name, title
nomino -are	to nominate
***non**	not
nonanus -a -um	ninth, of the ninth legion
***nondum**	not yet
***nosco, noscere, novi, notum**	to know, to get to know
nota -ae, f	mark
noverca -ae, f	step-mother
novercalis -e	belonging to a step-mother
***novissimus -a -um**	most recent, last
***novus -a -um**	new, novel, strange, recent
***nox, noctis, f**	night
noxius -a -um	guilty

nubes -is, f	cloud
nudus -a -um	bare
***nullus -a -um**	no, not any, none
***numerus -i, m**	number
***numquam**	never
***nuntio -are**	to announce
***nuntius -i, m**	messenger
nusquam	nowhere
nuto -are	to nod, falter
***ob (+ acc)**	for the sake of, on account of
obnitor -niti -nisus sum	to press against
oboedio, oboedire (+ dat)	to obey
obruo -ruere -rui -rutum	to bury, to overwhelm
obscurus -a -um	hidden, dark, secret
obsequium -i, n	obedience
***obsideo -sidere -sedi -sessum**	to beseige
obstringo -stringere -strinxi -strictum	to bind up, tie fast, to bind by oath
obtendo -tendere -tendi -tentum	to put forward as an excuse
obtestatio -onis, f	entreaty
obtestor -are	to call to witness
obtineo -tinere -tinui -tentum	to obtain
obtrecto – are	to disparage, criticise
obvius -a -um	in the way, in the path of
occulo -culere -cului -cultum	to cover up, conceal
occulte	secretly
occulto -are	to hide, conceal
occultus -a -um	secret
occurro -currere -curri -cursum	to run into
octavus -a -um	eighth
***octo**	eight
***oculus -i, m**	eye
***odium -i, n**	hatred
offendo, offendere, offendi, offensum	to offend
offensio -onis, f	offence, dislike
***offero, offerre, obtuli, oblatum**	to offer, present
officio -ficere -feci -fectum (+ dat)	to get in the way of
***officium -i, n**	duty

*olim	once
omen, ominis, n	omen
*omitto -mittere -misi -missum	to abandon, give up
*omnis -e	all, ever
onero -are	to burden, overwhelm
*onus -eris, n	burden
onustus -a -um	weighed down
*opes -um, f pl	material wealth
opperior -periri -pertus sum	to wait for
oppono -ponere -posui -positum	to put before, put against
*optimus -a -um	best
*opus -eris, n	work
*oratio -onis, f	speech
orator -oris, m	speaker
ordior, ordiri, orsus sum	to begin
*ordo -inis, m	rank, order
*orior, oriri, ortus sum	arise
*oro -are	to beg
osculum -i, n	kiss
*ostendo, ostendere, ostendi, ostentum	to show
ostentator -oris, m	demonstrator
ostento -are	to display
ostentus -us, m	show, display
*otium -i, n	idleness, free-time, quiet
paenitentia -ae, f	regret
*palam	openly
Palatium -i, n	the Palatine Hill in Rome
palor -ari	to wander
palus, paludis, f	marsh
Pannonia -ae, f	Pannonia
Pannonicus -a -um	Pannonian
*par, paris	equal
*parens -entis, m	parent, father
*pareo -ere	to obey
*pariter	equally
*paro -are	to make ready, prepare
*pars, partis, f	part, direction

particeps -ipis, c	sharer
parum	too little
*pater, patris, m	father, (pl) senators
*patior, pati, passus sum	to allow, suffer, endure
*patria -ae, f	country, homeland
*pauci -ae -a	few
*paulatim	gradually
*paulum	for a short time
paveo, pavere, pavi	to be frightened, tremble
pavesco -ere	to grow frightened
*pax, pacis, f	peace-time, peace
pecco -are	to make a mistake, go wrong, sin
pectus -oris, n	chest
*pecunia -ae, f	money
Penates -ium, m	Penates (household gods)
penitus	utterly
*per (+ acc)	through, at the hands of, in accordance with, by means of
per nomen	in the name of
percello -cellere -culi -culsum	to strike
perfero -ferre -tuli -latum	to carry out, deliver, endure
*perficio -ficere -feci -fectum	to accomplish, achieve
pergo, pergere, perrexi, perrectum	to be engaged upon, proceed, go on with
periculosus -a -um	dangerous
*periculum -i, n	danger
perinde	in the same way, equally
*permitto -mittere -misi -missum	to permit, to allow
permodestus -a -um	very modest, very moderate
*permoveo -movere -movi -motum	to stir up
permulceo -mulcere -mulsi -mulsum	to soothe, appease
pernotesco -notescere -notui	to become known
perpello -pellere -puli -pulsum	to push hard, drive, compel
perscribo -scribere -scripsi -scriptum	to write in full
perstringo -stringere -strinxi -strictum	to graze
pertimesco -timescere -timui	to be very scared

pervicacia -ae, f	persistence
*pes, pedis, m	foot
*pessimus -a -um	worst
*peto, petere, petivi, petitum	to seek, ask for
piaculum -i, n	any means of appeasing a deity, appeasement, remedy
placo, placare	to placate, appease, soothe
Planasia -ae, f	Planasia
plane	certainly, clearly
*plebs, plebis, f	common people, plebeians
*plerique, pleraeque, pleraque	most, the majority, very many
plurimus -a -um	most, very many
plus, pluris	more, (pl) many
*poena -ae, f	punishment
*pono, ponere, posui, positum	to put aside
*pons, pontis, m	bridge
pontificatus -us, m	Pontificatus (Rome's most important priesthood)
populor -ari	to lay waste, plunder
*populus -i, m	people
*porta -ae, f	gate
portendo -tendere -tendi -tentum	to portend, foretell
*posco, poscere, poposci	to demand
*possum, posse, potui	to be able
*post (+ acc)	after
*postea	afterwards
postpono -ponere -posui -positum	to put in second place
*postquam	after
postremo	finally, at last
postulatum -i, n	demand
*postulo -are	to demand, ask for
*potior -iri (+ gen)	to have control of
*potius	rather
*praebeo, praebere, praebui, praebitum	to offer, provide
praeceps -ipitis	headlong
praecipuus -a -um	especial, prominent, leading
*praeda -ae, f	plunder

praefectus -i, m	praefect, commander
praefectus castrorum	Praefect of the camp
praematurus -a -um	early, too early
praemitto -mittere -misi -missum	to send in advance
***praemium -i, n**	reward, prize
praescribo -scribere -scripsi -scriptum	to direct in advance, to outline
praescriptio -onis, f	title
***praesens -entis**	present, immediate
praesideo -sidere -sedi -sessum	I govern, am in charge
praesumo -sumere -sumpsi -sumptum	to apply beforehand
***praeter (+ acc)**	except
praetexta -ae, f	a toga with a purple border
praetoriae cohortes	the Praetorian Guard
praetorianus -a -um	praetorian, belonging to the imperial bodyguard
praetorius -a -um	belonging to a general/commander
praetura -ae, f	praetorship
praevenio -venire -veni -ventum	to anticipate
premo, premere, pressi, pressum	to suppress, cover, repress
prenso -are	to seize, grasp
prex, precis, f	prayer, entreaty
pridem	long ago, previously
primo	at first
primordium -i, n	beginning
primores -um, m pl	leaders
primum	at first
***primus -a -um**	first, foremost
***princeps -ipis, m**	First Citizen, *princeps*
principatus -us, m	Principate, rule
principium -i, n	beginning
***prior, prius**	earlier, former
priscus -a -um	former, ancient
privatus -a -um	private, belonging to an individual
privignus -i, m	step-son
***pro (+ abl)**	in place of, for
probo -are	to approve, prove
probrum -i, n	reproach

procax, procacis	shameless
proceres -um, m	nobles
procido -cidere -cidi	to fall down
procumbo -cumbere -cubui -cubitum	to sink down
***proelium -i, n**	battle
profero -ferre -tuli -latum	to extend, bring forth
***proficiscor, proficisci, profectus sum**	to set out
prohibeo -hibere -hibui -hibitum	to prohibit
proicio -icere -ieci -iectum	to cast out
proinde	consequently, therefore, just as if, just as
promiscus -a -um	indiscriminate
promo, promere, prompsi, promptum	to bring forth, produce
promptus -a -um	ready, prepared, quick
***prope**	near, nearly
propere	quickly
propero -are	to hurry
properus -a -um	hasty, quick, fast
propinquo -are	to approach
***propior, propius**	nearer, closer, rather resembling
prospere	favourably, successfully
prospicio -spicere -spexi -spectum	to take care, exercise foresight
prostremo	finally
protego -tegere -texi -tectum	to protect
prout	just as, according to
proveho -vehere -vexi -vectum	to carry forward, advance
provenio -venire -veni -ventum	to come about
provideo -videre -visi -visum	to think ahead, to take precautions for
***provincia -ae, f**	province
provisus -us, m	foresight, forethought
***proximus -a -um**	nearest, most recent
prudens, prudentis	sensible, experienced, intelligent
publice	in a public capacity, publicly
publicus -a -um	common, public
***pudor -oris, m**	sense of shame, modesty
puerilis -e	of a boy, youthful, childish
***-que**	and

quadrageni -ae -a	40 each
***quaero, quaerere, quaesivi, quaesitum**	to seek, ask for, look for
***quam**	than, how
***quamquam**	although
quamvis	although
***quando**	when, at some point, at the time when
***quantus -a -um**	to what extent, to which extent
***quasi**	as if
queo, quire, quivi, quitum	to be able
***queror, queri, questus sum**	to complain
questus -us, m	lament
***qui, quae, quod**	who, which, what
***quia**	because
quicumque, quaecumque, quodcumque	whoever, whatever, whichever
***quidam, quaedam, quoddam**	a certain
***quidem**	indeed
***quies -etis, f**	quiet, rest
quietus -a -um	at rest, sleeping
quin	indeed, but
quintadecumani -orum, m pl	soldiers of the fifteenth legion
quintusdecimus -a -um	fifthteenth
quippe	because, inasmuch as
***quis, quis, quid**	after *ne/si* – anyone, anything, any
***quis, quis, quid**	who, which, what?
***quisque, quaeque, quidque**	each, every
***quo**	to where, whither
quo	so that (introducing a purpose clause containing a comparative)
quo usque	how long?
quo minus	by which the less
quo minus	*introduces a clause of prevention*
***quod**	the fact that, because, since
quondam	once
***quot**	how many?
***quotiens**	whenever
quotus -a -um	how many in number?
***rapio, rapere, rapui, raptum**	to seize, carry off

rapto -are	to seize
***ratio -onis, f**	reason, account
***recens, recentis**	recent
***recipio, recipere, recepi, receptum**	to receive
***recito -are**	to read aloud
recondo -dere -didi -ditum	to store up
rector, rectoris, m	guide, instructor
recuso -are	to refuse
***reddo -dere -didi -ditum**	to deliver, to give back, return
***redeo -ire -ii -itum**	to return
redimo -imere -emi -emptum	to buy
redintegro -are	to renew
***refero -ferre -tuli -latum**	to take back, bring back, revive
regnatrix -icis	of a ruler, reigning
***regnum -i, n**	kingdom
***rego, regere, rexi, rectum**	to be king, to rule
regressus -us, m	return
reicio -icere -ieci -iectum	to refer
relatio -onis, f	report, proposal
***reliquus -a -um**	remaining, remainder
remedium -i, n	remedy
remeo -are	to return
reor, reri, ratus sum	to think, consider
***repente**	suddenly
reperio, reperire, repperi, repertum	to find
***repeto -petere -petivi -petitum**	to head back to, to seek again
requiesco -quiescere -quievi -quietum	to rest
***res, rei, f**	situation, thing, affair, fact, (pl) state of affairs
res capitales	capital offences
***resisto -sistere -stiti**	to resist
resolvo -solvere -solvi -solutum	to loosen, destroy
***respondeo, respondere, respondi, responsum**	to answer, reply
respublica, reipublicae, f	Republic
reticeo -ere	to be silent
retineo -tinere -tinui -tentum	to hold back, restrain, retain
reus -i, m	defendant

reverentia -ae, f	respect
revoco -are	to call back, bring back
Rhenus -i, m	the Rhine river
Rhodus -i, f	Rhodes
robur, roboris, n	strength
rogito -are	to ask repeatedly
*rogo -are	to ask
*Roma -ae, f	Rome
*Romanus -a -um	Roman
rudis -e	unskilled, untrained, inexperienced
rumor -oris, m	rumour, talk
ruo, ruere, rui, rutum	to rush, (of storms) to rage
*rursum, rursus	again
sacramentum -i, n	oath
saepio, saepire, saepsi, saeptum	to surround, fence in
saevio, saevire, saevii, saevitum	to rage, to be savage
saevitia -ae, f	savagery
*saevus -a -um	savage, cruel
salvus -a -um	unhurt, safe
sancio, sancire, sanxi, sanctum	to make sacred, confirm
sane	at any rate, certainly
*sanguis -inis, m	blood
sapientia -ae, f	wisdom, good sense
sarcina -ae, f	baggage
satietas -atis, f	satiety
*satis	enough, sufficient, sufficiently
saxum -i, n	rock, stone
*scelus -eris, n	crime
*scribo, scribere, scripsi, scriptum	to write
*se, sui, sibi, se	himself, herself, itself, themselves
semet	*intensified form of* se
sese	= *se*
secessus -us, m	retreat, withdrawal
secretum -i, n	secret
secretus -a -um	secret
securitas -atis, f	safety
*sed	but
*sedecim	sixteen

sedeo, sedere, sedi, sessum	to sit
***sedes -is, f**	base, resting place
seditio -onis, f	civil or military revolt, riot, uprising
***semel**	once
***semper**	always
sempiternus -a -um	everlasting, eternal
***senatus -us, m**	Senate
senectus -utis, f	old age
***senex -is, m**	old man
senilis -e	belonging to an old-man
sensus -us, m	feeling
***sententia -ae, f**	opinion
separo -are	to separate
sepelio, sepelire, sepelivi, sepultum	to bury
sepultura -ae, f	burial
***sequor, sequi, secutus sum**	to follow
sermo, sermonis, m	conversation, talk
servio, servire	to act as a slave, to be a slave
servitium -i, n	servitude, slavery, slaves (collective noun)
servitus -utis, f	servitude, slavery
***servo -are**	to keep
***servus -i, m**	slave
seu	or if, whether
severitas -atis, f	severity, strictness
***sex**	six
sextus decumus -a -um	sixteenth
***si**	if
sidus -eris, n	star, moon
signifer, signiferi, m	standard-bearer
***signum -i, n**	sign, signal, order, military standard
***silentium -i, n**	silence
***simul**	at the same time
simulatio -onis, f	pretence, hypocrisy
simulo -are	to claim falsely, pretend
sincerus -a -um	uncorrupt, sound
sine + *abl	without
singuli -ae -a	one (each), individual

*sive, seu	or if, whether
socio -are	to share
*socius -a -um	allied
*socius -i, m	companion
solitus -a -um	usual, accustomed
solor -ari	to console, comfort
*solus -a -um	only, alone
*solvo, solvere, solvi, solutum	to release, dismiss, pay
*sonus -i, m	sound, noise
*soror -oris, f	sister
*spatium -i, n	space, interval
species -ei, f	appearance
*specto -are	to look at, examine, test
*sperno, spernere, sprevi, spretum	to scorn, despire
*spes -ei, f	hope
spiritus -us, m	breath of life, spirit, breath
spiro -are	to breathe
splendidus -a -um	bright
sponte	of one's own accord
*statim	immediately
statio -onis, f	men positioned at a fixed location, guard, guard-post
*statuo, statuere, statui, statutum	to establish, decide
status -us, m	status, state, condition
sterilis -e	unfruitful
stipendium -i, n	pay (for a year's service), a year's military service
*sto, stare, steti, statum	to stand
stolide	stupidly, brutishly
strepo -ere -ui -itum	to make a loud noise, roar
struo, struere, struxi, structum	to engineer, arrange, erect
*studium -i, n	zeal, enthusiasm
*sub (+ acc / abl)	under, in the power of
subdo -dere -didi -ditum	to substitute falsely
subicio -icere -ieci -iectum	to subject
subnixus -a -um (+ abl)	resting on, supported by
subsidium -i, n	support, help
sufficio -ficere -feci -fectum	to be sufficient
*sum, esse, fui	to be

*summus -a -um	utmost, highest, most important
*sumo, sumere, sumpsi, sumptum	to take up
superbia -ae, f	arrogance
superbio -ire	to grow proud, arrogant
*supero -are	to overcome, survive
superstitio -onis, f	superstition
*supersum -esse -fui	to remain, be in existance
supplex, supplicis	suppliant, humble, submissive
supplicium -i, n	punishment
supra (+ acc)	beyond, above, over
supremus -a -um	final, last
*suscipio -cipere -cepi -ceptum	to undertake
suspecto -are	to suspect
suspectus -a -um	suspected, suspicious
suspensus -a -um	hesitant
suspicax -acis	suspicious
sustento -are	to strengthen, sustain
sustineo -tinere -tinui -tentum	to hold up, support
*suus -a -um	his/her/its/their own
tabernaculum -i, n	tent
*talis -e	of such a kind
*tam	so
*tamen	however, nevertheless
tamquam	as if
*tandem	at last
*tantum	only
*tantus -a -um	so great, so much, to such an extent, to that extent
tardus -a -um	slow
tegmen -inis, n	clothing
*tego, tegere, texi, tectum	to cover, hide
*telum -i, n	weapon
temero -are	to dishonour, defile
temperantia -ae, f	restraint
*tempestas -atis, f	time, season, storm
tempto -are	to attempt, to try
*tempus -oris, n	time, occasion

tendo, tendere, tetendi, tentum	to intend, to stretch out, to pitch (a tent)
tenebrae -arum, f pl	darkness
***teneo, tenere, tenui, tentum**	to hold, possess
tentorium -i, n	tent
***tergum -i, n**	back, rear
terminus -i, m	boundary
***terra -ae, f**	land, ground
***terreo -ere**	to terrify, frighten
***terror -oris, m**	terror, fear
theatralium operarum	a theatre claque (see notes)
tiro -onis, m	young solider, new recruit
toga -ae, f	toga
tolero -are	to endure
***tollo, tollere, sustuli, sublatum**	to take away, remove
***tot**	so many
totiens	so often
***totus -a -um**	whole
tracto -are	to pull about
***trado, tradere, tradidi, traditum**	to hand over, report, hand down
***traho, trahere, traxi, tractum**	to drag
tramitto -mittere -misi -missum	to pass over, send across
tranquillus -a -um	calm, peaceful
trepido -are	to be anxious
trepidus -a -um	frightened, anxious
***tres, tria**	three
tribunal -alis, n	speaker's platform
tribunicia potestas, tribuniciae potestatis, f	tribunician power
tribunus -i, m	tribune (6 in a legion)
tribuo, tribuere, tribui, tributum	to assign, bestow
tributum -i, n	tax, tribute
triceni -ae -a	thirty each
***tristis -e**	sad, dismal, harsh
triumphus -i, m	military triumph (i.e. the glory of special procession through Rome to denote an exceptional military victory)
trucido -are	to cut to pieces, to slaughter, to butcher

truculentus -a -um	savage, wild
trunco -are	to mutilate
trux, trucis	savage, grim
***tu, te, tui, tibi, te**	you (sg)
tuba -ae, f	trumpet
tueor, tueri, tutus sum	to watch over, protect
***tum**	then
***tumultus -us, m**	uproar
tunc	then
***turba -ae, f**	uproar, commotion, crowd, mob
turbator -oris, m	rabble-rouser
turbatus -a -um	disordered
turbo -are	to throw into uproar, disturb
turbo -inis, m	wind, storm
tutela -ae, f	care, charge, protection
tutor -ari	to protect, keep safe
***ubi**	where, when
uligo, uliginis, f	wetness
***ullus -a -um**	any
ultio -onis, f	revenge, punishment
ultra (+ acc)	further, beyond
umerus -i, m	shoulder
***umquam**	ever
***una**	together
***unda -ae, f**	flood-water, water
unicus -a -um	only, single
universus -a -um	all
***unus -a -um**	one, only
urbanus -a -um	of the city
***urbs, urbis, f**	city
urgeo, urgere, ursi	to press upon, to drive, to urge
usquam	anywhere
***usque**	all the way, up to
usurpo -are	to make use of
***usus -us, m**	use, need
***ut**	in order to, to, so that, that, when, as, how
utcumque	however

utilitas -atis, f	advantage, benefit, profit
*utor, uti, usus sum (+ abl)	to use
utrimque	on both sides
*uxor -oris, f	wife
uxorius -a -um	belonging to a wife
vacatio -onis, f	respite, exemption
vagus -a -um	roaming
valetudo -inis, f	health
*validus -a -um	strong
vallum -i, n	rampart
varie	in different ways
varius -a -um	various
*-ve	or
vectigal -alis, n	(indirect) tax
vehiculum -i, n	vehicle, carriage
*veho, vehere, vexi, vectum	to carry; (passive) to travel
*vel	or
*vel . . . vel	either . . . or
*velut	as if
*venio, venire, veni, ventum	to come
verber -eris, n	whip; (pl) lashing, beating
verbero -are	to beat
*verbum -i, n	word
vergo, vergere	to incline
*vero	indeed, in truth
*verto, vertere, verti, versum	to turn, overturn, change
*verus -a -um	true
vescor -i	to feed, eat
vespera -ae, f	evening
*vestis -is, f	clothing
veteranus -a -um	veteran
*vetus, veteris	old; (pl) ancestors
vexillum -i, n	military standard (i.e. the emblem which marked the different sections with the army)
*via -ae, f	road
*victor -oris, m	victor, conqueror
*victoria -ae, f	victory

vicus -i, m	village
*video, videre, vidi, visum	to see
vigeo -ere	to be strong, vigorous
vigiliae -arum, f pl	night guards
*viginti	twenty
vincio, vincire, vinxi, vinctum	to tie up
*vinco, vincere, vici, victum	to overpower, conquer, win
vinculum -i, n	chain
*vir, viri, m	man
*vis, vim, vi, vires, virium, viribus, f	violence, force, power
viso, visere, visi, visum	to go to see, visit
visus -us, m	vision, sight
*vita -ae, f	life
vitis -is, f	vine-rod, staff
*vix	scarcely
vixdum	scarcely yet
vocabulum -i, n	name, nickname
*voco -are	to call, summon
*volo, velle, volui	to wish, want
voluntas -atis, f	good will, will
*vos, vos, vestrum, vobis, vobis	you (pl)
votum -i, n	prayer
*vox, vocis, f	voice
vulgo -are	to make public, to make common, spread about
vulgus -i, n	mob
*vulnus -eris, n	wound
* vultus -us, m	facial expression

Index of Place Names

Index of Members of the Imperial Household

Index of Other Named Romans